Keeping Hearth and Home in Old MASSACHUSETTS

*K*eeping *H*earth and *H*ome in Old MASSACHUSETTS

A Practical Primer for Daily Living

compiled and edited by
Carol Padgett, Ph.D.

MENASHA RIDGE PRESS
BIRMINGHAM ✤ ALABAMA

Library of Congress Cataloging-in-Publication Data
is available from the Library of Congress

Cover design by Grant M. Tatum and Ann Marie Healy
Text design by Grant M. Tatum and Annie Long

Menasha Ridge Press
P.O. Box 43673
Birmingham, AL 35243
www.menasharidge.com

ISBN: 0-89732-408-0

*F*or

my mother
Dorothy Stiles Gillespie
1918–1995
who flavored her fare with inimitable flair

my grandmother
Myra McCord Stiles
1890–1967
*whose cornpones we still try to replicate
and whose life we still try to emulate*

my great grandmother
Emma McCord
1851–1925
whose nineteenth-century recipes for living have made all the difference

Contents

Acknowledgments

Attempting to assign proper measure to those who assisted in preparing this nineteenth-century buffet reminds me of my grandmother's efforts to leave her family the legacy of her cornpones. We were wise enough to request her recipe while she was in her cornpone prime, and she was kind enough to comply. Of course, she had no recipe. Trying valiantly to render one, she tossed each ingredient into a bowl, retrieved it by handfuls and pinches, and noted its proper measure with care. But, alas, there is no measure for a cook's intuition or the size of her palm. Our family has never replicated Ma-Mam's cornpones. We continue, however, to be richly nourished by the spirit of the cook.

Though I have shaped *Keeping Hearth and Home* at a keyboard rather than a pastry board with ingredients pulled from library shelves rather than kitchen shelves, the process has been reminiscent of growing up in Ma-Mam's kitchen. Menasha Ridge Press Publisher Bob Sehlinger invited me to gather the ingredients for this bill of fare and—with grandfatherly patience far beyond his years—hoisted me to the mixing bowl and entrusted me with the stirring spoon. He and editor Holly Cross have welcomed my handfuls and pinches with enthusiasm, tended my spills with tact, and monitored my pace toward "getting dinner in the oven" on time. Associate Publisher Molly Merkle prepared simultaneously for the delivery of my first book and her first baby and has moved between kitchen and nursery to nurture both. Menasha editor Nathan Lott stepped in to gather ingredients when I needed to turn my attention to other gardens. Developmental Editor Carolyn Carroll, bless her heart, culled our gleanings and arranged the buffet table with impeccable taste. Designer Grant Tatum added all the right touches to make it picture perfect. And Tricia Parks brought to the table her marketing genius to expand our efforts from a neighborly dinner into a cottage industry.

Ann Nathews, Library Director of Southern Progress Corporation, with the generosity of a neighbor offering a "starter batch," enriched our garden of ingredients with literary fodder stored in corporate silos. Sipping tea with a friend who approaches large gardens with aplomb was a fine way to ease into a daunting task! My husband Ben encouraged me to accept Bob's invitation by donning an apron, offering his personal and technological support, and purchasing a hand-held scanner. He has been a faithful "useful man," literally "taking care of the vestibule steps, the sidewalk and the porch area" because it makes me smile after a long day. From the other end of our marital computer table, he has added the secret ingredients of perspective and humor.

Donna L. McDaniel, a classmate from Tom Mullen's Writing Workshop at the Pendle Hill Quaker Retreat Center in Pennsylvania, took time from practicing her craft as a freelance journalist and editor in Southborough to serve as my Massachusetts research assistant. She was guided by Sarah Hutcheon and Kathy Herrlich of the Arthur and Elizabeth Schlesinger Library on the History of Women in America, Radcliffe Institute for Advanced Study, Harvard University. Carol Boulris of Needham, Massachusetts also contributed several interesting recipes. Joanne Lowry of Harvard, Massachusetts, home to a Shaker community from 1793 to 1918, was my rich resource for "all things Shaker." Carolyn Carroll provided extensive research for the recipes section and sidebar exerts, with the help of the Hartman Center for Sales, Advertising and Marketing History at the Rare Book, Manuscript, and Special Collections Library of Duke University.

Women of nineteenth century Massachusetts were my companions and mentors. Their recipes and "receipts," mores and maxims provide glimpses into the principles with which they nourished their relationships and the practices by which they ordered their lives. Their quaint language has stirred my heart; our hearthside conversations have seasoned my soul. As one of our forebears said upon presenting a similar book: "I have enjoyed the task heartily, and from first to last the persuasion has never left me that I was engaged in a good cause."

Introduction

Like her twenty-first century sister, the woman who kept hearth and home in nineteenth century Massachusetts juggled multiple roles. I have organized this book as a guide to fulfilling the functions those roles dictated in the realm of the home. Above all, the nineteenth century Massachusetts woman was "a lady," performing her duties and imbuing her activities with a lady's sensibilities. As the "lady of the home," she set the standards for its decorum; as keeper of the family, she orchestrated their enactment. As mistress of her household, she assured that her servants discharged their duties with dispatch and that her guests enjoyed the amenities associated with nineteenth century hospitality. She set her family table with pride and her company table with propriety, collecting the recipes that would make her meals delectable and the receipts that would make her silver shine.

This book is a lovingly constructed anthology of homemaking advice culled from a wealth of mid- to late-nineteenth-century cookbooks, household manuals, and periodicals. It is, in essence, a greatest-hits album of the domestic wisdom of the time, a simpler time, a time (for most Massachusetts women) without electricity, telephones, automobiles, supermarkets, and countless other conveniences we take for granted today. My passion for capturing the wisdom of this age resides in my lifelong fascination with the everyday lives of those who came before me: What was it like to live then? What were the tasks and pleasures that filled the hours of each day? I have always treasured the old-time literature of the home as a tender personal keepsake, much like the legacy of hand-written recipes and hand-stitched finery that my female predecessors left behind. For me, putting this book together was an opportunity to step into the shoes of my great grandmother, or even of her mother. I can see them sitting side by side, skimming these pages in search of just the right recipe for calf tongue, a trustworthy treatment for a colicky infant, or the best advice for making fine cologne water in anticipation of a rare night out.

I smiled and chuckled my way through the work of choosing the most representative pieces of advice to include. My mother, grandmothers, and all the great aunts, bedecked in their finest aprons and best memories, gathered in spirit 'round the hearth of my desk to help select and stir ingredients. We laughed at the measures and manners of yesteryear and lampooned the family legends of which they reminded us. Simultaneously 57 and 7, I rejoiced in the reverie of the childhood Sunday dinners that nourished our family with home-cooked food and touchstones of predictability—forks on the left, hands in the lap, elbows off the table, and my grandfather's weekly admonition to "count the silverware before taking out the trash." From the vantage point of my fifth decade, I relived my first: lips puckered to be glossed for a trip to town, eyes wide in search of "ladies" (who "could be spotted a block away by the presence of gloves"). Seventeen once more, I revisited reminders familiar to women of earlier eras: "It is just as easy to love a rich man as a poor man" or "Every young woman needs an education and skills to fall back on just in case."

It is my hope that *Keeping Hearth and Home* will stir your memories and bring the lives of your great or great-great grandmothers into the storytelling circle beside your family hearth, for this is how they lived. And this book is one they might have consulted, had such a comprehensive collection been available during their day. Instead, our forbearers consulted a variety of sources, learning about household management from "receipts" in the addenda of period cookbooks and learning the finer points of proper deportment and social propriety in the designated columns of weekly newspapers and in magazines such as *Godey's Lady's Book, Harper's Bazaar,* and *The Ladies Repository.*

These texts connected women to the broader society and assisted them in examining and shaping their individual lives. In fact, this literature became so extensive that *The Enterprising Housekeeper,* written in 1897, noted that it was "almost the fashion to apologize for taxing a much-abused public with the burden of a new book on this subject." Yet how grateful we should be for the abundance of this literature to educate us about the lives of our ancestors. How I have been humbled by this nineteenth-century wisdom, for so much of which our twentieth and twenty-first centuries have claimed credit.

It seems, more accurately, that women through the ages have agreed on a number of basic principles for orchestrating a home, harmonizing a marriage, and fine-tuning the children. As you shake your head at the quaintness of one practice—*A married gentleman shows respect for his wife by speaking of her as 'Mrs.' and never as 'my wife'*—or feel your skin prickle at the ignorance of outmoded mores—*A lady is at her best when she exhibits a modest and retiring manner*—you will also, surprisingly, often marvel at the modern-day wisdom of other instructions—*Better to live in one room, with all the furniture your own, than occupy a whole house with scarcely a chair or a table paid for.*

The mid-to-late-nineteenth century Massachusetts home existed in the larger context of a state that was thriving in endeavors as diverse as technology and transportation, leisure and letters. Massachusetts factories—specializing in woolens, cotton textiles, and leather tanning—kept a third of America in clothing and half of the country in boots and shoes. In two successive years during the 1870's, Massachusetts was the state in which the first American Christmas card was printed and the first telephone demonstrated. In the early 1890's Massachusetts introduced America to basketball in Springfield, and during three successive years in the mid-90's introduced volleyball in Holyoke, the public beach in Revere, and the subway in Boston. Immigration thrived as well, with European newcomers quickly replacing the numerous native laborers who left Massachusetts to move West.

Nineteenth century Massachusetts women made significant contributions in many spheres. A number of Bay State women of the period became famous for their intellectual and artistic accomplishments. Emily Dickinson (1830-1886), the noted American poet who is generally considered one of America's most important writers, lived in

Amherst; while Edith Wharton (1862–1937), the first woman to win a Pulitzer Prize for fiction, lived in Lenox. Celia Thaxter (1835–1894) of Newton was one of America's better-known women poets, and her works often appeared in popular monthlies of the time—the *Atlantic,* the *Independent, Scribner's* and *Harper's.* Louisa May Alcott (1832–1888) penned at Orchard House in Concord the 1868 classic *Little Women,* the first novel featuring juvenile female lead characters. Brookline native Theo Ruggles Kitson (1876–1932), one of the most prolific female bronze sculptors in America, created in a Farmington studio the allegorical and equestrian sculptures that still adorn communities across the state.

Nineteenth-century Massachusetts women are also known for their accomplishments in humanitarian service, education, and religion. Clara Barton (1821–1912) of Oxford, who founded the American Red Cross in 1881, began her work by advertising for donations of medical supplies and distributing them to Civil War battlefields with a mule team. Elizabeth Cary Agassiz provided leadership in 1879 for a nameless program known as "the Harvard Annex," later named Radcliffe College. Mary Baker Eddy (1821–1910), founder of the Church of Christ, Scientist and conceiver, at age 87, of the Pulitzer Prize winning *Christian Science Monitor,* stands as the only American woman to found a worldwide religion.

Massachusetts women also blazed trails in science, medicine, business, and architecture. Close to the heart of this book, chemist Ellen Swallow Richards (1842–1911), a sanitation and health advocate, pioneered home economics and environmental science by systematically remodeling an Italianate home in Boston's Jamaica Plain as a model of the highest standards of "right living." She designed windows to open at the top and bottom to release stale air, used indoor plants to produce oxygen, removed lead pipes, and re-routed the waste system to enhance hygiene. Richards, who had studied at the Massachusetts Institute of Technology as the first woman admitted to a scientific school, established there the first consumer home-testing laboratory, applying scientific principles to domestic economy and thereby redefining standards of household sanitation and efficiency. In 1862, Dr. Marie Zakrzewska

opened in Boston one of only a few hospitals in the country where female physicians could practice and perform surgery. Elizabeth Boit
(1849–1932) of Wakefield was the first female bank director in America
and one of the first female managers in the textile industry, where she
charted new territory by improving the working conditions of her em-
ployees. Lois Lilley Howe (1864–1964), an early champion of con-
fronting the problems of urban housing, was elected as the first female
fellow of the American Institute of Architects. In 1897, Edith Wharton
co-authored *The Decoration of Houses,* now considered one of the semi-
nal works of professional interior design.

Viewing nineteenth-century America through the prism of Massachusetts' famous suffragists reveals much about the role of women in
public life during the era. Elizabeth Cady Stanton (1815–1902) of
Seneca Falls and Susan B. Anthony (1820–1906) of Adams co-founded
in 1869 the National Women's Suffrage Association; Anthony was ar-
rested and fined $100 for breaking the law after she cast a ballot in the
1872 presidential election. Outspoken abolitionist and early suffragist
Abby Kelley Foster (1810–1887) and her husband Stephen Foster re-
fused to pay property taxes on their Worcester home, prompting a
succession of state auctions at which friends repeatedly purchased
Liberty Farm and returned it to the Fosters as a gift. Massachusetts
daughter Julia Ward Howe (1819-1910) was instrumental in so many
humanitarian efforts that it was said that "no movement or 'cause' in
which women were interested, from suffrage, to pure milk for babies,
could be launched without her. "Her famous "Battle Hymn of the Republic," composed to the cadence of "John Brown's Body," reportedly
caused Abraham Lincoln to cry.

Other views of Massachusetts women in the 1800's come from
glimpsing into the institutions that served them. The November
Club in Andover, for example, was the first New England structure
built as one of the women's clubs founded in almost every nineteenth-
century American town. The clubs served as meeting places, similar
to those enjoyed by the era's men, in which women engaged in literary and cultural exchange about issues of the day, such as suffrage,
temperance, and education. A final glimpse at nineteenth-century

customs comes from the only two requirements of the Berkshire Home for Aged Women in 1891: this fine Western Massachusetts retirement home in Pittsfield required only that applicants pay an initial fee of $300 and bring a black silk dress!

Amid the commotion of Massachusetts' thriving commerce and its lively, concerned community, the nineteenth-century home was a ship sailed to safety by the woman at its helm, and it was advice such as that preserved here that guided her work on the deck.

"If she shall thus succeed in disseminating a knowledge of the practice of the *most suitable system of domestic art known in our country*;

if she shall succeed in lightening the labors of the house-wife by placing in her reach a guide which will be found *always trusty and reliable*;

if she shall thus make her tasks lighter and home-life sweeter;

if she shall succeed in contributing something to the health of American children by instructing their mothers in the art of preparing light and wholesome and palatable food;

if she, above all, shall succeed in making American homes more attractive to American husbands, and spare them a resort to hotels and saloons for those simple luxuries which their wives know not how to provide;

if she shall thus add to the comfort, to the health and happy contentment of these, she will have proved in some measure a public benefactor, and will feel amply repaid for all the labor her work has cost."

—Marion Cabell Tyree
granddaughter of Patrick Henry
Lynchburg, Virginia, January 1877

 PART ONE

ℒady of the House:

GUIDELINES FOR PROPER DEPORTMENT

Chapter One

The Lady: Guidelines for Her Appearance and Demeanor

If the value of good breeding is in danger of being depreciated, it is only necessary to compare the impression which a gentle, pleasant demeanor leaves upon you with the gruff, abrupt, or indifferent carriage of those who affect to despise good manners. Indeed, society could not be maintained save for the usages of etiquette.

Her Personal Appearance

Always dress simply. A true lady does not adopt gay and showy colors and load herself down with jewelry which is entirely out of place and conveys a very great anxiety to "show off." Custom sanctions more brilliant colors in dress goods than formerly, but they should be selected with modifications for outdoor wear; quiet, subdued shades give an air of refinement and never subject their wearer to unfavorable criticisms.

Dress to enhance your finer qualities. It should merely be an appropriate frame for a charming picture, bringing out the beauties of the picture but never distracting attention from it. So few women understand this. Your dress may, or need not, be anything better than calico; but, with a ribbon or flower or some bit of ornament, you can have an air of self-respect and satisfaction that invariably comes with being well dressed.

SELECT SIMPLE ACCESSORIES. Never carry coarse embroidered or laced handkerchiefs. Fine, plain ones are much more ladylike. Avoid open-worked stockings and very fancy slippers. For special occasions, fine, plain white hose and black kid slippers with only a strap of rosette in front are more becoming.

SCENT YOUR ACCESSORIES NOT YOURSELF. Procure a small quantity of *poudres aux fleurs*—which is common hair powder scented with flowers and is to be procured at any perfumer's—fold it in an envelop so that it cannot escape, and lay it in the drawer appropriated to laces, gloves, and handkerchiefs, which will acquire from it that faint, scarcely perceptible odor which is so pleasing. Scented French glove boxes are sufficient in themselves, sometimes, for all necessary purposes; and, if a liquid be used, let it be as sparingly as possible. I only seek to impress upon my lady friends the truth of the old proverb as applied to perfumes: "Too much of a good thing is good for nothing."

SUIT YOUR BONNET TO YOUR FACE. If one has a long, slender face, the bonnet should be arranged to make a soft framing; while if one has a broad, full face, the bonnet should be sufficiently large, and its trimmings arranged to give a high rather than a wide effect. Ties should always be worn, even if they have to be very narrow because of a plump throat. Nothing gives a woman quite so ridiculous an air as an unsuitable bonnet fastened on like that worn by a girl of seventeen, and with the hair flying all about.

AVOID THE TIGHT BODICE OR SKIRT, IF STOUT. The average dressmaker who attempts to make a gown for a stout woman makes it as close fitting as possible—as bare of trimming as can be. Nine times out of ten, even if she makes the sleeves full at the top, she fits them in below the elbow, so that every particle of flesh on the arm is held down, and the hands are extremely red. The result of a tight-fitting bodice is a red face, and, consequently, the stout woman should not wear one, but instead should select that which, while it fits her well, also permits every ounce of flesh to stay in its proper place.

Equally unbecoming to her is a tight-fitting skirt. For that reason, one with not only a little fullness around the top, but with a fold or two arranged across the front is advised. The stout woman should remember that trimmings carried up to the shoulder, high sleeves, and bretelle effects all have a tendency to increase the height, and that should be her aim in dressing.

MAKE OF YOUR SLENDERNESS A BEAUTY. Wear a bodice that tends to make your shoulders look broader and a much-trimmed skirt that gives to you height and presence. About your waist there must be no trimming, so that its natural smallness can be brought out.

SPORT QUIET COLORS. New or bizarre colors are considered the privilege of the extremely young woman. Flaring blues, brilliant greens, glowing pinks, or deep yellows seldom look well on a middle-aged woman. She can always wear the rich, deep colors; and that she is being catered to nowadays is shown by the popularity of royal purple, of deep petunia, and of the daintiest grays imaginable. Black and white are always in good taste.

In Silk and Lace

By 7 o'clock Mrs. Gray was in her corner, dressed in black silk, with purple ribbons in her cap, and some fine knitting in her hand. Catherine, a brunette, wore a pink silk fastened with black-velvet rosettes, and with puffed sleeves of black Spanish lace. Clara's dress was white cambric striped with pale green. She wore in her hair sprigs of the pale smilax; an old-fashioned gold chain, with a square, red-jeweled ornament, clasped her slender throat, and long ear-rings.

—Elizabeth Stoddard, "The Tea-Party," 1871

Her Personal Demeanor

CARRY YOURSELF WITH GRACE. The beauties of the charming picture framed by one's dress are enhanced by moving with grace. To walk with style is rare enough, but when it comes to being able to sit down in a dress properly—well, there are not many equal to that, I can tell you.

KEEP YOUR ARMS FROM GOING ASTRAY. A question often comes up, not so easily answered: What shall I do with my hands and arms? Some ladies carry a fan. But you cannot always have one in your hands, so it is better to keep the arms pressed lightly against the sides in walking or sitting. This position for the hands, although a little stiff at first, will soon become easy and graceful. Ladies should never adopt the ungraceful habit of folding their arms or of placing them akimbo.

Dress Modestly Outside the Home

BE GRACEFUL IN YOUR MANNERS. A lady should be quiet in her manners, natural and unassuming in her language, careful to wound no one's feelings, but giving generously and freely from the treasures of her pure mind to her friends. She should scorn no one openly but have a gentle pity for the unfortunate, the inferior, and the ignorant, at the same time carrying herself with an innocence and single-heartedness that disarm ill nature and win respect and love from all. Such a lady is a model for her sex, the "bright particular star" on which men look with reverence. The influence of such a woman is a power for good that cannot be overestimated.

Her Demeanor in Social Exchanges

LIMIT YOUR OBSERVATIONS. A boisterous, loud-talking man is disagreeable enough, but a woman who falls into the habit is almost unendurable. Many times have we seen an inoffensive husband tucked completely out of sight by the superabundant flow of volubility proceeding from a wife, who, we like to believe, is by nature intended to be the gentler and restraining element.

BE NOT EXCESSIVELY FRANK. Do not take pride in offensively expressing yourself on every occasion under the impression that you will be admired for your frankness. Speaking one's mind is an extravagance, which has ruined many a person.

ALWAYS ACCEPT APOLOGIES. Only ungenerous minds will not do so. If one is due from you, make it unhesitatingly.

LISTEN. When a "tale of woe" is poured into your ears, even though you cannot sympathize, do not wound by appearing indifferent. True politeness decrees that you shall listen patiently and respond kindly.

LAUGH AT THE APPROPRIATE TIME. Don't laugh when a funny thing is being said until the climax is reached. Do not laugh at your own wit; allow others to do that.

USE TACT WHEN ADMONISHMENT IS NECESSARY. Tact is needed in a friend to show us our weaknesses; also with employers and parents. How many do harm instead of good in their manner of rebuking, wounding instead of rousing the self-respect of those they reprimand!

REFRAIN FROM EYEING OVER OTHER WOMEN. Few observant persons can have failed to notice the manner in which one woman, who is not perfectly well bred or perfectly kind hearted, will eye over another woman, whom she thinks is not in such good society and, above all, not at the time being in so costly a dress as she herself is in. Who cannot recall hundreds of instances of that sweep of the eye, which takes in a glance the whole woman and what she has on from top-knot to shoe-tie. It is done in an instant. No other evidence than this eyeing is needed that a woman, whatever be her birth or breeding, has a small and vulgar soul.

TREAT ENEMIES KINDLY. If you have an enemy and an opportunity occurs to benefit the person in matters great or small, do good service without hesitation. If you would know what it is to feel noble and strong within yourself, do this secretly and keep it secret. A person who can act thus, will soon feel at ease anywhere. If enemies meet at a friend's house, lay aside all appearance of animosity while there and meet on courteous terms.

KISS SPARINGLY. Many times a contagious disease has been conveyed in a kiss. The kiss is the seal of pure and earnest love and should never be exchanged save between nearest and dearest friends and relatives. Indeed, public sentiment and good taste decree that even among lovers it should not be so often indulged in as to cause any regret on the part of the lady should an engagement chance to be broken off. Let promiscuous kissing, then, be consigned to the tomb of oblivion.

GREET FRIENDS WITH DISCRETION. A lady does not call out to friends or inquire after their health in a boisterous fashion. Ladies do not rush up to each other and kiss effusively. It is a foolish practice for ladies to kiss each other every time they meet, particularly on the street. It is positively vulgar; a refined woman shrinks from any act that makes her conspicuous. Such practice belongs rather to the period of "gush" natural to very young girls and should be discouraged on physiological grounds, if no other.

CHAPTER TWO

THE HOSTESS: GUIDELINES FOR SPONSORING HER SPECIAL GATHERINGS

We feel certain that it will help the novice or the timid one to know just what to do to avoid those breaches of etiquette which almost always draw ridicule upon the offender. Such breaches betoken a want of acquaintance with the manners of refined life.

Developing Experience in Hosting Multiple Guests

Confine your first entertaining efforts within small bounds, beginning with few dishes, a very simple service, and a small number of guests; as you gain the confidence, which follows frequent efforts, you can safely extend your hospitality.

Start Simply

STUDY TO LEARN. Study established customs in the best-managed houses you visit; take counsel with experienced friends; now and then make modest essays on your own responsibility, and, insensibly, these crumbs of wisdom will form into a comely loaf.

Favors Save the Cotillion

*U*pon the favors, quite as much as upon the leader, the success of a cotillion depends. Many dances, which would otherwise have gone down in the history of society events as dull, have been redeemed by them. The popularity of a hostess rests largely upon her ability to provide surprises for her friends—a succession of them—continuing all through the german, thus holding her guests until the last figure has been danced.

Although at some of the fashionable dances favors claim a large share of the expense, they need not necessarily be costly. Novelty and daintiness are the only qualities they must possess. They should show the forethought of the hostess, to whom appropriateness should be the watchword, and they should also be well balanced—that is to say, the same style of favors should not be provided for the different figures. They should vary, those for one figure being large, those for the next small.

—*Harper's Bazar,* 1905

LIMIT AMBITION TO ABILITY. Exercise sufficient good sense to limit your social ambition by your ability to carry out your plans. It is adequate to offer perfectly quiet entertainment, the requirements of which come within the capacity of your household.

START WITH A PARTY. We make this matter of company too hard a business in America. Parties are less troublesome to a housekeeper than dinners because they are less ceremonious. If you can afford it, the easiest way to give a large one is to put the whole business into the hands of the profession by entrusting your order to a competent confectioner. But a social "standing supper" of oysters, chicken salad, sandwiches, coffee, ice-cream, jellies, and cake is not a formidable undertaking when you have had a little practice, especially if your mother or the nice, neighborly matron over the way will assist you by her advice and presence.

CONSIDER THESE NEW POPULAR PARTIES:

☒ A pretty device is to make of your lawn party a *flower party*. For these, some particular flower is chosen, and all the floral decorations consist entirely of these.

☒ An *apple-blossom party* will be new to most. Steal from the trees the precious blossoms to make large bouquets, headdresses, and parasols for the young ladies in attendance. Adorn the tables with great bunches of apple blossoms, and present each guest with a spray tied with Nile-green ribbon. The hostess should likewise wear a dress of Nile-green looped with apple-blossoms.

☒ *Tennis parties* are somewhat novel, and because they take place in the day time, they may partake somewhat of the nature of an afternoon tea. These parties are informal, as the players are in tennis costume. The invitations need not be confined to those who play, for tennis is a game that is greatly enjoyed by onlookers.

☒ If you host an *afternoon out-of-door tea,* know that it is customary for the hostess to wait on the guests herself. If she requires any assistance, a few friends may help her. Everything should be as dainty as possible, with the finest china and prettiest doilies. The refreshments may be very simple.

The Children's Party

It is well to give children from the beginning, and in their everyday life, some practical ideas of the duties of a host or hostess to see that the company has a good time. The child in whose honor the party is given must cut the cake and serve it to the others, if he or she is old enough to know how to attend to it.

PLAN AND DIRECT THE PLAY. The matter of playing ought always to be supervised by the hostess. It is a good plan to make little program for the evening and keep it well in hand, dropping anything that does not "take" and ready with another to put in its place. Dancing, games, and riddle-guessing are among the recreations.

HAVE CHILDREN DRAW PARTNERS FOR SUPPER. Drape several long strings—half the number of party guests—around the room, in a criss-cross formation to create a cobweb effect. Each child finds one of the free string ends and begins untangling the web until they are connected to the child at the other end of their string—their intended partner.

GAMES TO ATTEMPT:

☞ *Contradiction.* Four children hold a handkerchief by its corners. One stands by them who commands their movements. But the game is *contradiction:* therefore, when she says, "Hold fast!" they drop the handkerchief; when she cries, "Let go!" they must hold it tightly. In *obeying* the order given, they must pay a forfeit.

☞ *Blowing Out the Candle.* This play affords a great deal of amusement. A lighted candle is placed on a table; the player is blindfolded and whirled several times round to make him lose his bearings. He will probably not walk toward the table at all; or, if he does, will make ridiculous efforts at blowing out the candle from want of preciseness of proximity.

☞ *"Roll Over, Come Back."* One of the games chosen over and over again is "Roll over, come back! So merry and free, My playfellow dear, Who shares in my glee!" The children sit in a circle and one child from the center rolls the ball, usually a wooden one, to each of the children in turn, all singing the song. Later, two children roll from the center, then three, and finally four. This requires quick wits and close attention and never seems to pall. The words can easily be set to home music, but Eleanor Smith's song book No. 2 contains the most satis-factory tune we have yet had.

☞ *Squirrel Game.* All stand in a circle but two little squirrels, who have a hole away off by themselves somewhere. One squirrel runs out and touching somebody's clasped hands leads him a lively chase before running back to the hold. If he is caught he is put inside the ring which is supposedly a cage, and the one who caught him becomes a squirrel. When two or more are caught they are fed nuts and then set free.

Guidelines for Hosting a Dinner

She who would give a dinner, which shall be a joy to gentle people, must know the art of combining arts; proportions in light, color, food, sound, perfume, fabric, finance, ware, diplomacy, brotherly love—she will need to use them all.

Preparation

SELECT GUESTS CAREFULLY. Much tact and thoughtfulness is necessary in choosing the guests for a dinner. Not only should social obligations and personal preferences be consulted, but also the individual characteristics of the guests; for a disagreeable neighbor can destroy the entire enjoyment of a repast whose guests are placed in close proximity for hours.

PROCURE BOUTONNIERES AND CORSAGES FOR THE GUESTS. In summer each gentleman may be supplied with a *boutonniere* and each lady with a corsage bouquet. The bouquets are tied with ribbons of contrasting colors, and a large pin is stuck into the cloth for the purpose of fastening the flowers to the dress. At elaborate entertainments, when it is desired to present the ladies with some souvenir, bouquet clasp pins may be substituted for the ordinary large pin or the large pin may be made of gold or silver. Very pretty silver pins can be bought for from fifty cents to one dollar, and more fanciful ones and bouquet pins for from one dollar upwards, according to their style of ornamentation.

LAY THE TABLE WITH THE FOLLOWING:

-❧ Upon the left, a soup spoon and two silver forks, one large.

-❧ In the center, the dinner-plate, upon which the plate of oysters or clams is to be set with the oyster fork just before serving the dinner; or, if there is to be no shellfish, the napkin may be put here with the dinner bread.

-❧ At the right of the cover, a steel knife with a pearl or ivory handle, for meats, and a silver dinner knife of medium size, as well as sometimes a smaller knife with a silver blade and some fanciful handle, to be used for cheese, salad, or butter when it is served, as it generally is upon American tables.

⁂ When the shellfish is served, the bread and napkin may be laid just above the spoon and forks together with the saltcellar and water-tumbler or the small *carafe* with the tumbler reversed upon it.

⁂ Napkin rings should never be used, save in the strict privacy of home; for it is an open secret that the use of a napkin ring suggests repeated use of the napkin—a practice highly improper with guests.

⁂ When wine is served, the glasses may be symmetrically arranged at the upper right of the cover.

⁂ The number of wineglasses is, of course, regulated by the variety of wines to be served.

⁂ Individual saltcellars are in vogue, but several larger silver or cut-glass ones may be placed upon the table, as well as some unique and pretty pepper casters of metal or china.

⁂ The salad oil and vinegar are in double cruet-stands upon the table or on the sideboard ready to be placed upon the table when the salad is served.

⁂ Individual water bottles, with tumblers to cover them, are much favored because of their convenience to this water-drinking nation. Dishes of broken ice are permissible at small dinners. The water bottles may be filled with ice and frozen without much trouble. Some caterers make a specialty of supplying these frozen *carafes*.

STOCK THE SIDEBOARD. Include plenty of fresh napkins, plates, cups and saucers for coffee, dessert dishes, finger-bowls, sugar, cigars or cigarettes when there are gentlemen present, and wines and *liqueurs,* which are not iced. The teaspoons are upon the sideboard, to be placed upon the table when required. Small spoons are needed when coffee is served in the little cups used after dinner for black coffee, or *café noir.* When there is not an abundance of silver, there should be, in a room adjoining the dining room, all the conveniences for quickly washing and drying it.

Before the Meal

The social duties of the hostess are too clearly defined to admit of any deviation from them.

WELCOME GUESTS APPROPRIATELY. At least half an hour before the time named for dinner, the hostess should be dressed and ready to receive her guests, although they are not expected to arrive much before the dinner hour. Her place should be near enough the door to permit her to welcome each one who enters. To the ladies she says a pleasant word and establishes them comfortably, chatting with them between the arrivals; to every gentleman she at once indicates the lady whom he is to take in to dinner, introducing him if the parties are strangers.

INSPECT THE TABLE. Before dinner is served, the hostess should snatch a moment, if possible, to inspect the table in person or instruct a trustworthy factotum to see that everything is in place. If it is a gentleman's dinner, she can see to it for herself, since she will not be obliged to appear in the parlor until a few minutes before they are summoned to the dining room. If there are ladies in the company, however, she must not leave them.

During the Meal

ENTER AND SEAT PROPERLY. Ordinarily the gentleman who is the guest of honor goes into the dining room last, with the hostess, and is seated at her right. The servant draws out the chair of the guest of honor, or that of the lady whom the host escorts. If there are attendants

Evening Parties

*A*n evening party is a scene redolent with beauty and fashion; the air is sweet with the mingled perfumes of thousands of lovely flowers, arranged in baskets, vases, flat dishes, festoons, wreaths, and also in beds of mosses and ferns.

—Marion Harland, *A Manual of Etiquette with Hints on Politeness and Good Breeding*, 1873 enough, the chairs of all the guests may be drawn out, and replaced by the attendants as the guests are seated. When there are not enough servants to place the chairs, each gentleman assists the lady he escorts.

CONVERSE LIGHTLY. All dinner talk should be light and amusing, but even commonplace conversation is more acceptable than silence.

ALLOCATE SERVING DUTIES PROPERLY. If the serving be done by the host and hostess, the host serves the substantial dishes, and the hostess the tea or coffee, vegetables or entrees, puddings, and the dessert. Where there are servants to do the waiting, the hostess should serve the soup, salad, dessert, and coffee; the host, the fish and meat; and the servants, the vegetables and entrees.

PREPARE THE TABLE BEFORE DESSERT. When the last course is done, crumbs must be removed or the table cloth changed. The dessert plate, containing a finger bowl and dessert knife and fork, is then set before each guest, who at once removes to the table the finger bowl and its doily and the knife and fork, leaving the plate ready for dessert. Sometimes a small glass containing a little perfumed water is set in the finger bowl; at the end of dinner, this glass is raised to the lips to refresh them, and the fingers are dipped into the bowl.

FOLLOW YOUR GUESTS OUT OF THE ROOM. At the close of the dinner, the hostess bows to the lady at the right of the host, for whom the host rises and opens the door. She leads the way out of the dining room, the other ladies following her, and the hostess going last; this, of course, is at large formal dinners, otherwise there is no special-form imperative.

A Fine Meal is Essential for Any Dinner Party

Menu for Full-Course Dinner

Blue Points.

Consommé à la Royal.

Olives.   Celery.   Salted Almonds.

Swedish Timbales with Chicken and Mushrooms.

Fried Smelts.   Sauce Tartare.   Dressed Cucumbers.

Saddle of Mutton.   Currant Jelly Sauce.

Potatoes Brabrant.   Brussels Sprouts.

Supréme of Chicken.

Mushrooms à la Sabine.

Canton Sherbet.

Canvasback Duck.   Olive Sauce.

Farina Cakes with Jelly.

Celery Salad.

Apricot and Wine Jelly.

Nesselrode Pudding.   Rolled Wafers.   Parisian Sweets.

Crackers.   Cheese.

Café Noir.

For a gentlemen's dinner, canapés accompanied with sherry wine are frequently served before guests enter the dining room.

At a ladies' luncheon, the courses are as many as at a small dinner. In winter, grapefruit is sometimes served in place of oysters; in summer, selected strawberries in small Swedish Timbale cases.

—*Boston Cooking-School Cook Book*, 1896

Following the Meal

ATTEND TO ALL. In the drawing room, the hostess should always chat a little with all her guests, even if the number is large; but she should pay special attention to strangers.

Last night I went to Mrs. Wise's Musicale & afterwards to a large dancing party given by Miss Coleman. This latter was the party of the season & Cousin Lucy was especially anxious for me to be there. I wore my white silk & looked unusually gorgeous. Miss Coleman has the reputations of giving the most select entertainments in the city & it certainly appears to be true. The whole house was thrown open & brilliantly illuminated. We (the Executive party) arrived about 10 p.m. & found the rooms comparatively empty; but, about half past 10 the rush began & by 11 p.m. the rooms were full, though not too crowded for comfort. The ballroom had an inlaid floor & was waxed to the last degree of slipperiness.

At 12 supper was announced & never in my life have I seen such a beautiful & elegant table. Terrapin, rare wines, costly French dishes, delicious ices, etc., etc. It is not my habit to eat much at a party but I really ate more there than ever before.

—Lucy Scott West's firsthand account of her stay at the
White House during the Hayes Administration, 1878

ARRANGE FOR ENTERTAINMENT. If there is any lady present accomplished in any way, the hostess may request her to assist in entertaining the others; and compliance on the part of the guest should be immediate and cheerful unless there is some grave reason for declining. The hostess may omit such requests for assistance without implying any offence. In the case of guests who are professionally distinguished, this question of entertainment should always be previously understood, because sometimes there are objections to their contributing to the evening's amusement. Guests who are amateur musicians should commit a few pieces to memory; if they carry music along it has an appearance of conceit, but if they are asked to play or sing it is ungracious to refuse.

My wife, I will not deny, was a little elated at the idea of having a city editor to dinner; but when I repeated, one by one, your extraordinary expectations, she became very thoughtful and silent.

Why you see, sir, the "spring chickens" we could count upon, by-and-bye; but the "trout," the "woodcock," the "snipe," the "wild ducks," and, coolest of propositions, that all these should be brought on consecutively, keeping half a dozen cooks busy, and quite confounding my father and my dear old aunt with such unheard-of proceedings—all these, and ices, and wines, in our quiet country home—Oh, sir, I blush at the thought of it. Moreover, I withdraw the invitation. Don't come to dinner. I forbid it.

—S. H. Hammond and L. W. Mansfield,
Country Margins and Rambles of a Journalist, 1855

OBSERVE COURTESIES AS THE EVENING CLOSES. After the gentlemen enter the drawing room, tea should be served, and then the guests are at liberty to depart. As each guest takes leave of the hostess, a few words should be said in acknowledgment of the enjoyment of a pleasant evening, without any reference to the dinner itself.

CHAPTER THREE

———•———

THE HOSTESS:
SPONSORING HOUSE GUESTS

Guidelines for Hospitality

WELCOME THEM SIMPLY. Welcome the coming guest with a few, simple, pleasant, easy words; without ostentatious cordiality; without gushing declarations of friendship; without paralyzing his arm by an interminable shaking of hands; without hurry, flourish, due anxiety to have his trunk carried up to his room, or sandwiching between every sentence an anxious appeal to make himself entirely at home—an appeal which usually operates to make one feel as much away from home as possible.

AVOID ESPIONAGE. The constant taking for granted that the guest is not comfortable and that the host and his family must hurry about and take all responsibility from the guest, thus depriving him of the credit of common sense, is something worthy of indignation—all the more so because politeness forbids the least sign of impatience. It is erroneous to presume that, unless you establish a kind of espionage over your guest and watch his every movement, you will be wanting in courtesy.

REQUEST NOTIFICATION OF A VISIT. Do not be ashamed to say to your nearest of kin or the confidante of your school days, "Always let me know when to look for you." If you are the woman I take you to be—methodical, industrious, and ruling your household according to just and firm laws of order and punctuality—you need this notice.

PREPARE FOR HER. It only requires a little closer packing of certain duties, an easy exchange of times and seasons, and leisure is obtained for the right enjoyment of your friend's society. A home prepared looks thus:

The additional place is set at table. Your spare bed, which yesterday was tossed into a heap so that both mattresses might be aired, is made up with fresh sheets that have not gathered damp and must from lying packed beneath blankets and coverlets for maybe a month for fear somebody might happen in to pass the night and catch you with the bed in disorder. The room is bright and dustless. Towels are in plenty, fresh soap is in the dish, fresh ink in the inkstand, fresh pen in the holder, stationery at hand, and the pin cushion well supplied with pins. Candles and matches and water are on the stand by the bedside. The drawers of closet and bureau are empty and, if sachets are not supplied, smooth white paper is spread in them. The dainty dish is prepared for dinner or tea so as to be "off your mind." Your husband knows whom he is to see at his homecoming. The children are clean and on the qui vive—children's instincts are always hospitable.

The guest's welcome is given in the air of such a house. Perhaps, as she lays aside her traveling dress, she smiles at your "ceremonious, old-maidish ways" and marvels that so good a manager should deem such forms necessary with an old friend.

RECEIVE UNANNOUNCED VISITORS HAPPILY. Since unexpected visitors will occasionally drop in upon the best-regulated families, make it your study to receive them gracefully and cordially. If they care enough for you to turn aside from their regular route to tarry a day, night, or week with you, it would be churlish not to show appreciation of the favor in which you are held. Make them welcome to the best you can offer at so short notice, and let no preoccupied air or troubled smile be token to your perturbation.

PUT UP LUNCHEON UPON THEIR DEPARTURE. It is a graceful act to provide a pasteboard box of lunch for a departing visitor, as during a long journey the opportunities for a comfortable meal are often lacking. Most ladies, myself among the number, would usually prefer to go without a dinner than to hurry to the counter of a railway dining saloon, give an order, and attempt to eat and drink with one eye on the clock and the other on the cars.

Receiving Your Husband's Guests

Especially, let your welcome be ready and hearty when your husband brings home an unexpected guest.

WELCOME HIS GUESTS GLADLY. If he can walk home, arm in arm, with the schoolfellow he has not seen before in ten years, not only fearlessly, but gladly anticipatory of your pleasure at the sight of his; if, when the stranger is presented to you, you receive him as your friend because he is your husband's, and seat him to a family dinner, plain but nicely served, and eaten in cheerfulness of heart; if the children are well behaved and your attire that of a lady who has not lost the desire to look her best in her husband's eyes—you have added to the links of steel that knit your husband's heart to yours.

SERVE AS YOU WOULD ALWAYS. The majority of healthy men have good appetites and are not disposed to be critical of an unpretending bill of fare. The chance guest of the male sex is generally an agreeable addition to the family group, instead of do trop—always supposing him to be your husband's friend.

CHAPTER FOUR

---

*T*HE LADY AS GUEST, CALLER, CORRESPONDENT

The Lady Guest

There is the art, too, of making oneself agreeable as a guest.

NOTIFY YOUR HOSTESS IN ADVANCE. Laying to your conduct the line and plummet of the Golden Rule, never pay a visit (I use the word in contradistinction to "call") without notifying your hostess-elect of your intention thus to favor her. Perhaps once in ten thousand times, your friend—be she mother, sister, or intimate acquaintance—may be enraptured at your unexpected appearance, traveling satchel in hand, at her door to pass a day, a night, or a month. But the chances are so greatly in favor of the probability that you will upset her household arrangements, abrade her temper, or put her to undue trouble or embarrassment, that it is hardly worth your while to risk so much in order to gain so little.

ADAPT YOURSELF. Endeavor to conform, without apparent effort, to the arrangements of the family with whom you board and to the manners and customs of the people around you, as far as they do not compromise your principles of good morals and good taste. If you don't like a thing, let it alone; eat nothing, and by the next meal you may be glad to eat anything.

AVOID DINING RUDENESS. Blowing soup or pouring tea and coffee into the saucer to cool it evidences a lack of knowledge of the usages of good society. Beware, lest you make that disagreeable sound in eating soup which is not only offensive to the ear but is a positive rudeness. Do not eat all on your plate and do not clean it up with your bread. In a dinner of several courses, it is unusual for a guest to ask for any dish a second time.

RECIPROCATE YOUR HOST'S WELCOME. A dinner invitation should always be returned during the social season—that is, before people separate for the summer. If the recipient has not an establishment, which admits of giving a dinner in return, a ride or drive in the country, a good restaurant dinner, or a theatre party in the city is considered a social equivalent.

The Lady Caller

Calls cement the acquaintance with all whom you admit to your circle.

REMEMBER THE IMPORTANCE OF CALLING. Formal calls in the city are intended to serve in lieu of the more genial and lengthy visits, which are a part of country life. Calling is the surest way to maintain agreeable acquaintances and foster those friendships that brighten life.

CALL AT THE PROPER TIMES. Morning calls are not, as their title would imply, calls made in the forenoon but embrace the hours from 1 to 5 p.m. They are generally of 15 or 20 minutes in duration. Calls in the evening are made from 8 to 9 p.m. and should be of an hour's duration. A gentleman whose time is his own can call between 2 and 5 p.m. But, as business engrosses nearly all our gentlemen, from 8 to 8:30 in the evening is the proper time to make a social call. If he calls before that hour, he may interfere with some previous engagement his hostess may have, and will surely displease her by his eagerness. Dress suits are for evening calls.

CALL FOLLOWING A REVERSE. If a friend has met reverses and you desire to show your friendship by visiting her, do not go dressed expensively. Adapt your dress to her changed circumstances.

DEPORT YOURSELF PROPERLY DURING CALLS.

- ⚜ Sit quietly in the place the servant has assigned you, and rise when the hostess enters.

- ⚜ While waiting in the parlor for the lady on whom you call to appear, the piano must remain untouched, as also the bric-a-brac.

- ⚜ The outer wraps are retained while making calls, the brief time allowed for remaining making it unnecessary to remove them.

- ⚜ In making a ceremonious call, a gentleman's hat and cane are retained in his hand and his gloves remain on, but an umbrella is left in the hall.

- ⚜ Do not enter into grave discussions; trifling subjects are better.

- ⚜ It is not customary to partake of refreshments during calls.

☞

Some Points on Etiquette

If when making a social call a second visitor arrives, the first caller, if she has made a call of sufficient length, should after a few minutes take her leave. When calling, if a lady finds several persons have preceded her, she should invariably greet the hostess first, ignoring all others until this courtesy is shown.

—Earl S. Sloan, *Sloan's Cook Book and Advice to Housekeepers*, 1905

❧ Do not draw near the fire when calling, unless invited.

❧ If strangers are in a room when a caller leaves, a slight bow in passing out is sufficient recognition.

The Proper Use of the Calling Card

A calling card is but a bit of pasteboard and would seem to be of no consequence, and yet it is a silent messenger, which vouches for the cultivation and familiarity with good usages of its owner.

SEND CARDS TO ACKNOWLEDGE AN INVITATION. When an invitation to a church wedding or a marriage announcement is received, it is necessary to send cards to those in whose name it was issued and to the newly-married pair. It is bad form to write "regrets" or "accepts" on a card; a note of reply must be written in acknowledgement of an invitation.

SEND CARDS TO NOTIFY OTHERS OF ABSENCE. When leaving town for a protracted absence, P.P.C. cards are sent. The initials P.P.C. stand for the French words *pour prendre conge* (meaning to take leave) and are always in the lower right-hand corner of the card and in capitals.

OBSERVE CARD ETIQUETTE FOR MARRIED COUPLES. Married men are relieved from the task of making calls of ceremony. The wife leaves her husband's card in lieu of a call. The custom is for a married woman calling formally on another married woman to leave one of her own and two of her husband's cards, one of his being for the hostess and the other for her husband.

OBSERVE OTHER CARD ETIQUETTE. Do not examine the cards in the card basket. You have no right to investigate as to who calls on a lady. In large cities, it is usual to leave cards when attending an afternoon tea. Those who are in mourning should have cards with a black border. A business address should never be seen on a visiting card. A card with a photograph on it is a piece of vulgar conceit.

The Lady Correspondent

REGARDING PARTICULAR LETTERS:

☞ Letters of introduction are used to introduce one friend to another who lives at some distance. Do not give a letter of introduction to anyone with whom you are not thoroughly acquainted. Such letters are generally left unsealed, and the name of the person introduced should be written on the lower left-hand corner of the envelope in order that the persons on meeting may greet each other without embarrassment.

☞ Letters of friendship or letters among very intimate friends admit of less formal terms, such as Very sincerely yours, Your dutiful son, Your affectionate nephew, etc. The chief essentials in letters of friendship are that the style be simple and the manner of expression be natural; it is the incidents of everyday life, the little things, the home chat that make a friendship letter interesting.

☞ Never write a letter when you are laboring under great excitement, for you will almost certainly write things that you will repent next day. When constrained to write severe things, the letter should be permitted to lie over night for review before mailing. If this be done, it is probable that the character of the letter will be changed radically, or perhaps it will remain unwritten. Many letters which would seem ample provocation for a sharp reply had better go unanswered. Kind words make and hold friends, while hasty or vindictive words alienate friends.

☞ Letters of courtesy include invitations, acceptances, letters of congratulation, of condolence, of introduction, and of recommendation, all of which are more formal in style than letters of friendship.

☞ To write a good love letter you ought to begin without knowing what you are going to say and finish without knowing what you have written.

☞ To write a letter of congratulation on mourning paper is rather inconsistent.

LETTER WRITERS SHOULD REMEMBER:

☞ No gentleman or lady ever writes an anonymous letter.

☞ Do not fill your letters with apologies and mere repetitions.

☞ Avoid writing with a pencil or with other than black or blue-black ink.

☞ Letters about one's own affairs, requiring an answer, should always enclose a stamp, to pay return postage.

☞ Short sentences are easier to write than long ones, hence more suitable for correspondence.

☞ The signature should be written very plainly, for no matter how familiar your intimate friends are with your dashing ink lines, others may have considerable difficulty in associating them with your printed name.

☞ In social correspondence, the envelopes, like the paper, should be white and plain and should correspond to the paper used in size and quality. It is considered bad taste to use colored paper or other than black ink.

☞ Be sure to write to a friend, or hostess, after making a visit at her house, thanking her for her hospitality. Don't wait a fortnight before doing so.

☞ It is the fault of the English language that we have so many "bad spellers." If you are doubtful of a word, it will be better to look it up rather than make a blot, or a running line, where the letters are questioned. Careful reading, and lots of it, will make a good speller.

CHAPTER FIVE

———•———

*T*HE LADY IN MOURNING

Funeral Etiquette

DRESS THE DECEASED SIMPLY. In dressing the remains for the grave, those of a man are usually "clad in his habit as he lived." For a woman, tastes differ; a white robe and cap, not necessarily shroud-like, are decidedly unexceptionable. For young persons and children, white cashmere robes and flowers are always most appropriate.

USE FLOWERS SPARINGLY. A few flowers placed in the dead hand—perhaps a simple wreath—is plenty, but not those unmeaning memorials, which have become to real mourners such sad perversities of good taste and such a misuse of flowers. Let those who can afford to send such things devote the money to the use of poor mothers who cannot afford to buy a coffin for a dead child or a coat for a living one.

FOLLOW PROPER PRACTICE WHEN DEATH IS CAUSED BY DISEASE. Bodies of persons dying of smallpox, scarlet fever, diphtheria, membranous croup, or measles should be wrapped in several thicknesses of cloth wrung out of full-strength corrosive sublimate, carbolic, or formaldehyde solution and should not thereafter be exposed to view. The funeral should be private and no persons except the undertaker and his assistant, the clergyman, and the immediate family of the deceased should attend. Carriages used by persons attending the funeral ceremony should be fumigated. No person should enter the sick room until it has been thoroughly disinfected.

PREVENT BURYING A LOVED ONE ALIVE. Since there are no reliable methods for determining death and since new chemical and industrial methods of putting people in comas are multiplying in society, the fear of burial alive is very real. There have been reports of corpses exhumed with hair and nails grown long and fingernail scratches in the coffin lid. The reader is directed to a recently patented improved burial case. The nature of this invention consists in placing on the lid of the coffin, and directly over the face of the body laid therein, a square tube, which extends from the coffin up through and over the surface of the grave, said tube containing a ladder and a cord, one end of said cord being placed in the hand of the person laid in the coffin, and the other end of said cord being attached to a bell on the top of the square tube; so that, should a person be interred before life is extinct, he can, on recovery to consciousness, ascend from the grave and the coffin by the ladder; or, if not able to ascend by said ladder, ring the bell, thereby giving an alarm and thus save himself from premature burial and death; and if, on inspection, life is extinct, the tube is withdrawn, the sliding door closed, and the tube used for a similar purpose.

Mourning Practices

FOLLOW THIS ETIQUETTE WHEN IN MOURNING:

☞ *A widow's mourning* should last 18 months. The color of black for heavy mourning should be a dull dead hue, not a blue-black nor yet with any brown shade. For the first six months, the dress should be of crape cloth or Henrietta cloth covered entirely with crape, collar and cuffs of white crape, a crape bonnet with a long crape veil, and a widow's cap of white crape if preferred. After six months' mourning, the crape can be removed and grenadine trimmings used, if the smell of crape is offensive, as it is to some people. After 12 months, the widow's cap is left off and the heavy veil is exchanged for a lighter one. The dress can be of silk grenadine, plain black gros grain, or crape-trimmed cashmere with jet trimmings, and crepe lisse about the neck and sleeves. *Bows, flowers, and decorative finishing* generally are wholly out of place in deep mourning; lace and embroidery are wholly inadmissible.

⚜ *The veil* is always of crape and in this country is worn very long—most inconveniently and absurdly so, indeed. This fashion is very much objected to by doctors, who think many diseases of the eye come by this means. The crape also sheds its pernicious dye into the sensitive nostrils, producing catarrhal disease as well as blindness and cataract of the eye. It is a thousand pities that fashion dictates the crape veil, but so it is. It is the very banner of woe, and no one has the courage to go without it. We can only suggest to mourners wearing it that they should pin a small veil of black tulle over the eyes and nose and throw back the heavy crape as often as possible, for health's sake.

⚜ *Mourning for a father or mother* should last one year. A deep veil is worn at the back of the bonnet, but not over the head or face like the widow's veil, which, when down, covers the entire person.

⚜ *Mourning for a brother or sister, for step-father or step-mother, and for grandparents* may be the same as for the parents, but the duration may be shorter.

⚜ The period of *mourning for an aunt or uncle or cousin* is of three months' duration.

⚜ Wives and husbands wear mourning for the relatives of their spouses.

⚜ *Mourning for children* should last nine months. In the first three months, the dress should be crape trimmed, the mourning less deep than that for a husband. No one is ever ready to take off mourning; therefore these rules have this advantage—they enable the friends around a grief-stricken mother to tell her when is the time to make her dress more cheerful, which she is bound to do for the sake of the survivors, many of whom are perhaps affected for life by seeing a mother always in black. It is well for mothers to remember this when sorrow for a lost child makes all the earth seem barren to them. *Servants* are usually put in mourning for the head of the family—sometimes for any member of it. They should wear a plain black livery and weeds on their hats; the inside lining of the family carriage should also be of black.

The Graves of Friends

As we drove home he said: "I believe that I know every grave in the old villages within a radius of 30 miles from Boston. I search out the histories of these forgotten folk in records and traditions, and sometimes I find strange things—oh, very strange things! When I have found out all about them they seem like my own friends, lying there forgotten. But I know them! And every spring, as soon as the grass begins to come up, I go my rounds to visit them and see how my dead men do!"

—Rebecca Harding Davis, *Bits of Gossip,* 1904

PART TWO

The Mistress of Her Household

CHAPTER ONE

—◆—

*F*URNISHING AND DECORATING HER HOME

The greatest part of one's life is spent indoors, and the surroundings and decorations of our particular abode tend to make our existence either more sober-faced or mirthful in countenance.

The Importance of Thoughtful Appointment

KNOW THE RESULTS OF YOUR SELECTIONS. Furniture, decorations, and other surroundings that are disorderly or in bad taste have a harmful effect on the character of a home's inmates. The worst effect is upon the impressionable minds of growing children, who naturally take their own homes as models; what they see in childhood tends to fix their standards for life. Hence, neat, tasteful, and orderly homes—but not necessarily expensive in their appointments—have a very important educational influence.

MODEL TASTE AFTER NATURE. Follow nature and good taste will not be offended. Do not encourage shams; let everything be genuine. Do not substitute the grotesque for the graceful or make a sacrifice of comfort to carry out an idea. Do not paint wood to imitate bronze or plaster to look like stone. Remember that there is an eternal fitness in things. Comfort and taste can easily be combined.

KEEP YOUR HOME IN ORDER. To beautify one's home and freely use it is a duty we owe to the innate love of beauty God has implanted in us:

- ❀ Plant trees for shade and fruit; cultivate flowers and shrubbery.
- ❀ Keep up the fences, and keep the house painted.
- ❀ If a gate hinge or a door knob be broken or out of order, repair it at once; let nothing "go to rack."
- ❀ Adorn your house with books, pictures, and papers, and enliven it with music.
- ❀ There is no folly in this, but the best wisdom. Your life will be happier and doubtless longer, and your children will grow up more refined and contented, cherishing a stronger affection for you and an attachment to the home that will make them cling to it and to you when old age comes on.

The Front Room

Let the front part of the house be thrown open and the most convenient room in it be selected as the family room. Let its doors be ever open; when the work of the kitchen is completed, let mother and daughters be found there with their appropriate work. Even if the family living-room be plain, the children leave traces of their growing up in it, and the faces of the old people who have there lived out their lives look down from its walls.

DRESS APPROPRIATELY. Let no hat ever be seen in that room on the head of its owner; let no coatless individual be permitted to enter it. If father's head is bald—and some there are in that predicament—his daughter will be proud to see his temples covered by the neat and graceful silken cap that her hands have fashioned for him. If the coat he wears by day is too heavy, calicoes are cheap, as is cotton wadding.

Miracle of Neatness

…every room was miracle of neatness. Some of them were furnished in the fashion of Mrs. Gray's early days, and the remainder modernized by Clara's taste. She was fond of flowers; her windows were full of pots, and flower-stands were everywhere; she bought books also novels and poems. Chintz was a weakness with her, and comfortable cushions prevailed, and covered furniture; in short, the whole house had an individual atmosphere pleasing to all.

—Elizabeth Stoddard, *"The Tea-Party,"* 1871

OUTFIT THE ROOM WITH A READING AREA. Let that table, which has always stood under the looking glass against the wall, be wheeled into the room, its leaves raised, and plenty of useful—not merely ornamental—books and periodicals be laid upon it. When evening comes, bring on the lights, and plenty of them, for sons and daughters, all who can, will be most willing students. They will read; they will learn; they will discuss the subjects of their studies with each other; and parents will often be quite as much instructed as their children.

DECORATE THE ROCKING CHAIR. The ugly back of a splint rocking chair can be improved by covering it with a strip of drab linen with a narrow border in outline stitch on each edge. Slip one end between the strips of wood at the top, bring the other end under at the bottom, and fasten them securely. They may be kept in place by tying them to the rounds at the top; this looks pretty if done with ribbons.

DECORATE THE GENTLEMAN'S CHAIR. A pretty way to cover the upper part of the back of a handsome chair is with a towel of fine quality and heavily fringed ends. Tie the center of the towel with a ribbon or cord tightly so that the ends of the towel are left hanging like the ends of a necktie; put the tied center of the towel in the middle of the back of the chair and spread the ends out, putting a bow of ribbon at the center where the towel is tied. This is particularly tidy for a gentleman's high-backed chair, as he may lean his head on either side without soiling the chair.

DECORATE THE WALLS EASILY. The cover designs and full-page illustrations of several of the leading monthly and other periodicals are reproductions of the best works of prominent artists and illustrators. These are freely used in many homes to decorate the walls of libraries, dens, and sometimes living rooms, either framed or bound in *passe-partout* binding or merely neatly trimmed with a straight edge and attached to the wall by means of brass-headed tacks or thumb tacks. A series of cover designs of one or more periodicals makes a very interesting and attractive frieze for the den or library.

CONSIDER CALLERS WHEN TIDYING. As a last finishing touch to the parlor, leave late papers, magazines, a volume of poetry, or a stereoscope and views where they will be readily picked up by callers.

The Dining Room

Of all rooms in the house, the dining room should be cheeriest, because it is where all members of the family are most likely to congregate. No matter how widely the interests and occupations of father, mother, and children may separate them at other times of the day, at least one-fifth of their waking hours will probably be spent at the table.

USE FURNITURE FIRST. In fitting the dining room, its capacities should be studied. Unless there is ample space, no superfluous ornamentation should be attempted; all desirable room should be given to the necessary furniture. Here, a list of furniture recommended:

▨ *Table.* The table should be firm and solid and not so shaky that guests may fear some catastrophe. Decidedly, square and round tables are the most desirable; because, placed in a circle or nearly facing the host, no guest is given precedence except those who occupy the seats of honor at the right hand of the host and hostess respectively.

▓ *Chairs.* Chairs upholstered with leather are the nicest, and oak chairs with high backs are popular. Chairs can be made absolutely comfortable with practicable cushions; small hassocks can be placed under the table for additional comfort. Cane-seat chairs should never be used in the dining room; they catch beads and fringes and play sad havoc with them. The perforated wood ones are equally bad; the brass-headed nails with which they are fastened catch worse than the cane.

▓ *Serving tables.* A side table for carving will be needed. This carving table can be mounted on rollers so that it can be brought near the dining table when it is required. The sideboard may be of any fancied design which affords the convenience of shelves for plate and table ornaments, and drawers and under-closets for linen, cutlery, plate, and fine glassware. The drawers used for plates and the under-closets should be provided with locks.

▓ *China closet.* The china cabinet is a useful and beautiful article of furniture, but in the absence of such a cabinet any ordinary closet opening into dining room may be utilized by replacing its door with a decorative door with diamond panes of glass or with a drapery hanging from a rod and drawn aside when the dining room is in use.

▓ *Looking glass.* When a looking glass or mirror is used, either as part of a sideboard or for wall decoration, care should be taken that no rays of sunlight strike it; their chemical action destroys the perfect distribution of the amalgam with which the reverse of the glass is coated and causes an appearance of granulation or crystallization upon the surface of the mirror.

ONCE FURNITURE IS PLACED, DIVERT YOUR ATTENTION TO ENHANCING THE ROOM'S ATMOSPHERE:

⬤ *Install ample sources of well-placed light.* The ideal dining room is bright with sunlight or lamplight; if it is possible to admit sunshine to the dining room, it should be done. In the country, enjoy the delight of an outdoor dining room upon the piazza or lawn. In cities, dependence must be placed upon neutral-tinted walls and draperies, enlivened by freshly colored pictures, the light of open fires, and the soft colors of candle flame and shaded lamps. If there can be only one open fire in the house, put it in the dining room.

Clean Windows Regularly

⊛ *Wall hangings.* Many dining rooms are furnished with dark wood; the walls are gloomy or covered with dismal pictures of dead game and fish. Instead, let the pictures be of fruit or of other still life with bright colors. The most modest establishment admits these possibilities, and from them the plainest repast gains a charm.

⊛ *Rugs.* The floor may be bare. Indeed, a wooden floor with one or more rugs is preferable to a carpeted floor. Woolen fabrics attract and retain odors, especially those arising from heated fat. For this reason, as well as upon the score of cleanliness, a movable carpet or rug is better for dining room use than one nailed to the floor.

⊛ *Window decorations.* There can be no more appropriate or enjoyable window decoration than that of stained or painted glass; the infinite variety in form and coloring offered in artistic and lovely designs makes an embarrassment of riches in this form of decoration.

Window draperies should temper but not exclude air and sunshine. When the outlook of dining room windows is upon blank walls and paved yards, the unsightly prospect may be hidden, while permitting the free passage of light and air, by using Madras muslin curtains. Figured lace, cheesecloth, or sheer nettings with dried fern or autumn leaves gummed upon them will serve this purpose.

⊛ *Decorative china.* When fine china or old pieces of plate are used in decorating the dining room, they should be disposed above the doors and fireplace on shelves or brackets.

Sleeping Rooms

PROVIDE SEPARATE BEDS. Where two persons sleep in the same bed, the one who has the stronger physical power is likely to absorb the vital forces from the weaker one. Where either is afflicted with any tendency to consumption, skin disease, or another malady, he is likely to impart its evil influences, if not its actual contagion, to the person who shares his bed.

OUTFIT BEDS WITH:

▣ *Bed slips.* Bed linen often falls short of covering the mattress completely while in use; hence, the extra slip is needed, especially to protect from dust the underside of the mattress. These slips can be removed and laundered twice a year or oftener when housecleaning; the pillow covers may be removed oftener if desired. Ticking treated in this way will be fresh and clean at the end of a dozen years' hard usage, when otherwise it would be so worn and soiled as to be unfit for use.

▣ *Linen sheets.* Linen is, of course, the best material for comfort, appearance, and durability, but cotton sheeting is more commonly used because it is less expensive. Buy unbleached linen or cotton for sheets and pillow slips, as it is not only less expensive, but much more durable and can be easily bleached when laundered.

▣ *Feathers.* The best feathers for beds and pillows are feathers plucked from live birds. Chicken, goose, or duck feathers may be preserved and used for beds or pillows by putting all the soft feathers together in a barrel as they are picked from the birds. Leave the barrel open to the sun and rain, covering it with an old screen to prevent the feathers from blowing about.

▣ *Pillow sham holder and lifter.* The holder consists of a light frame readily attached to any bedstead, upon which the shams are pinned or sewn to a tape and are held in their proper position during the day, either with or without a pillow under them. At night, by means of a spring, they are instantly raised up against the headboard of the bed, entirely out of the way of the sleeper.

PROVIDE FOR VENTILATION. There is a superstition prevalent in many parts of the country that night air is injurious. In most localities this notion is entirely groundless and misleading. If we do not breath night air at night, pray what shall we breath? Either it is necessary to breath over and over the air that has been in the sleeping room all day or else to admit fresh air from outdoors, and whatever the danger in breathing night air, it is certainly less immediate than quick or slow suffocation from lack of ventilation.

SLEEP OUT OF DOORS IF POSSIBLE. Probably no practice would be more invigorating, healthful, or pleasurable than sleeping out of doors. In the vicinity of the great sanitariums, where sleeping out of doors has been proved to be a cure for consumption and other diseases, many persons have formed the habit of sleeping thus. Any porch somewhat excluded from view and in a sheltered location can be utilized. The porch should be screened and provided with storm curtains of tent canvas that can be drawn and buttoned like the curtains of a carriage. If the porch is used during the day, a bunk or folding bed may be hinged to the wall on one side, with legs that will let down on the other. When folded up this may be concealed by a waterproof curtain. Or one of the so-called hammock beds may be suspended by hooks from the ceiling.

Consider a Hammock for Your Porch

[49]

CHAPTER TWO

———•———

$\mathcal{A}$PPOINTING YOUR KITCHEN

There are very few housekeepers indeed who could not—by intelligent forethought in planning and arranging the kitchen, pantry, and storeroom—save themselves daily miles of useless traveling to and fro.

Furniture

BEGIN WITH THE CORRECT FURNITURE:

* *Stove.* First, the housekeeper must have a good stove or range, and it is well for her to have the dealer at hand when it is put up, to see that it draws well. A piece of hard, smooth asbestos board under the range, cook stove, parlor stove, gas stove, or small oil stove is superior to iron or zinc because it is durable, easier to keep clean, and presents a better appearance. The woodwork near stoves and the collars above stovepipes, where they pass through the ceiling and side walls, may be protected by the same material.

* *Ovens.* Separate ovens, set apart, should be used for meat and pastry because the particles of fat which fly from the meat while it is baking burn upon the sides of the oven and impart their odor and flavor to delicate cakes and pastry. The bread and pastry ovens do not

require to be so hot as those in which meat is baked, and means must be devised to moderate their heat when it is excessive. All the flues, and the top and bottom of the ovens, should be kept free from ashes, and the dampers should always be in good working order.

❀ *Sink.* The sink may be of iron or another metal, stone, or even wood lined with lead, tin, or zinc. But it should stand on four legs. The sink should be placed high enough so that the dishes may be washed without stooping. A small shelf or cupboard above the sink to contain soap, borax, washing powder, and various utensils will be found convenient.

❀ *Sink-side work table.* A bench or table, homemade if necessary, at the left of the kitchen sink and as large as the room will admit is indispensable.

❀ *Tableware cabinet.* Placing a china cabinet for the ordinary tableware just above the sink-side work table saves time and steps lost in walking from the sink to the table and thence to pantry or closet.

A Kneading Table Can be Very Useful

✸ *Stool.* Provide a strong stool, high enough to sit on, at the sink to pare vegetables and for other purposes.

✸ *Work table.* The kitchen table may be used as a work table if covered with oilcloth. This will last a long time if the table is padded with sheet wadding or several thicknesses of newspaper covered with an old sheet. Draw the padding smooth and tack it under the edge of the table.

✸ *Kitchen cabinet.* A good kitchen cabinet with metal bins for flour, meal, and other substances that mice are fond of is an investment which will save time and strength for the housekeeper and will be a money saver in the long run. These bins should be removable, so that they can be regularly washed, scalded, and dried.

✸ *Footstool.* A footstool, convenient also as a receptacle, may be made of a common pine soap box; fasten the cover on the box with small hinges

Elevators at Home

Elevators from kitchen to dining room are very common, but not any more important than one from cellar to pantry. It can be made with 3 or 4 shelves, using plank for end pieces, and will be better if made with a back of wire cloth, with doors in front, having the same covering in the place of panels, the same as safes for victuals, then the woman can place her victuals therein and lower to the cellar without going down at all, and raise when wanted for the next meal. If a wife is worth saving, have one put in at once, and she will bless you, as well as the day you had it done. Make as light as possible to be stout enough for the purpose. Any good mechanic can do it.

—A.W. Chase, *Dr. Chase's Third Last and Complete Receipt Book and Household Physician,* 1903

and put on the bottom four small castors. Line the box with plain white paper and cover. Excelsior, available at any furniture store, is good to stuff the top and much cheaper than curled hair.

✱ *Bread-warming shelf.* If you can have a three-cornered shelf of slate or sheet-iron placed in a corner of the kitchen just above the bread block, it will be all the better; though a common wooden shelf, made very thin, will answer where you can not get the other. A coal-oil lamp underneath will keep bread gently heated all night and will answer the double purpose of keeping a light burning, which most persons like to do at night and which they can do with scarcely any expense by using a coal-oil lamp.

Other Useful Objects to Have About

FOR YOUR OWN OR YOUR COOK'S CONVENIENCE, PROVIDE YOUR KITCHEN WITH:

➤ *Washboard.* Hang beside the sink a small washboard to rub out dishcloths and keep towels clean.

➤ *Slate.* A child's school slate hung on a nail, with a slate pencil attached by a strong cord, will be found a great convenience in ordering groceries. When any supplies run low, make a note on the slate of what is wanted; when the grocer calls, run over this list to refresh your mind. The slate is also useful for making a program each morning of the things to be done through the day. You will be surprised to find how quickly these things will be disposed of. When cooking or preparing company dinner, make a list of the articles to be prepare.

➤ *Toppers.* Keep a *nice flat washed rock* to weigh down butter, beef, or tongues under brine, and *stiff writing paper* to dip in brandy and lay on top of preserves.

➤ *Sleeve protectors.* An old pair of stockings may be converted into useful sleeve protectors by cutting off the feet and hemming the cut edge. These may be drawn over the sleeves of a clean gown when washing dishes.

➤ *Dishcloths.* Save and use cloth flour sacks, sugar, salt, and cornmeal bags, which keep white and last longer than ordinary towel stuff. You may also use scrim or cotton underwear crocheted about the edge or folded and hemmed double or the fiber of the so-called dishrag gourd, the seeds of which may be obtained from any seedman. Cheesecloth is good both for washing and wiping dishes, especially for drying silver and glassware.

➹*Match safe.* Keep a stock of matches on a high, dry shelf in a covered earthen jar or tin box where they will be out of the way of children and safe from rats and mice. These animals are fond of phosphorus and will gnaw match heads if they can, often setting them on fire.

➹ *Ash receptacle.* Keep a sheet-iron pan or scuttle to take up ashes.

A Cheery Home

To a passer-by the domain presented a cheerful view; order was established everywhere. The sun shone on a bright-painted walls, the windows glittered, the grassy bank beneath them was newly mown and spotted with the petals of the snowbell-bushes, growing beside the high granite steps. The firs on the lawn were fluried with the breeze, and Clara's pansies and tulips trembled in the flowing airs. Hens clucked in the garden, and scrambled after a man who was turning up the clods. The necessary cat, instigated by the song of a robin, scampered up and down the palings, watched by a big dog, who lay on the terrace, his paws crossed in lazy content.

—Elizabeth Stoddard, "The Tea-Party," 1871

The Store Room

Groceries and supplies for a household of any size should, if possible, be bought in quantity. Therefore, every house should have a store room, appointed as follows.

Cleaning and Voting

Housewives: You do not need the vote to wash out your sink spout... Good cooking lessens alcoholic craving quicker than a vote... Why vote for pure food laws when you can purify your ice box with saleratus water.

—A pamphlet published by the Women's Anti-Suffrage Association of Massachusetts

MAKE A STORE ROOM INEXPENSIVELY. A small storeroom can be made in a corner of the cellar at much less cost than is commonly supposed by putting up walls of concrete made of sand or gravel and cement. When furnished with a suitable door, this storeroom will be damp-proof and free from dust, germs, and all other unsanitary pests. There should be a cellar window protected on the outside by wire netting and having on the inside a removable screen of cheese cloth to keep out the dust. If you would have wholesome food, keep the window down at the top, night and day, except in the coldest weather.

INCLUDE AMPLE SHELVING. Slat shelves painted with white paint and a coat of enamel may be built up in a storeroom back to back, with just enough room between them for a person to walk, in the same manner as book stacks in a library. Preserves, pickles, butter, eggs, and other groceries can be stored year round in perfect safety.

HANG NETS FOR FRUIT. A suspended net or two should also be supplied for hanging lemons and oranges.

STOCK THE ROOM WITH EARTHENWARE. Earthenware jars are necessary for sugar, oatmeal, rice, tapioca, sago, barley, and spices. And, if one wishes to keep on hand the pound cake and fruit cake of our grandmothers (some cakes made from old-fashioned recipes given in this book will keep for years), no snugger quarters for their preservation can be found than earthen jars with tight-fitting lids.

Housekeeper's Alphabet

Apples—Keep in dry place as cool as possible without freezing.

Brooms—Hang in the cellar to keep soft and pliant.

Cranberries—Keep under water in the cellar; change water monthly.

Dish of hot water set in oven prevents cakes, etc., from scorching.

Economize time, health, and means, and you will never beg.

Flour—Keep cool, dry, and securely covered.

Glass—Clean with a quart water mixed with tablespoon of ammonia.

Herbs—Gather when beginning to blossom; keep in paper sacks.

Ink Stains—Wet with spirits turpentine; after three hours, rub well.

Jars—To store and protect.

Keep an account of all supplies with cost and date when purchased.

Love lightens labor.

Money—Count carefully when you receive change.

Nutmegs—Prick with a pin, and if good, oil will run out.

Orange and lemon peel—Dry, pound, and keep in corked bottles.

Parsnips—Keep in ground until spring.

Quicksilver and the white of an egg will destroy bedbugs.

Rice—Select large grains with a clear look; old rice may have insects.

Sugar—for general use, the granulated is best.

Tea—Equal parts of Japan and green are as good as English breakfast.

Use a cement made of ashes, salt, and water for cracks in stove.

Variety is the best culinary practice.

Watch your back yard for dirt and bones.

Xantippe was a scold. Don't imitate her.

Youth is best preserved by a cheerful temper.

Zinc-lined sinks are better than wooden ones.

—*Centennial Buckeye Cookbook*, 1876

KEEP AN ACCOUNT BOOK. In the store room, you should enter the date when each store is bought and the price paid for it in your account book.

MAKE AN OUTDOOR CUPBOARD AS WELL. Have you an outdoor cupboard in which to keep milk, meat, and fish during the cool weather of early spring and fall? A dry goods box with a hinged locked door, nailed above the reach of cats and dogs against the arbor that covers the kitchen door, will save many a journey to the store room. It should have holes bored in the ends to allow a current to circulate through it, for food will keep fresher and sweeter in the open air.

The Kitchen Garden

I wish all my fair sisters would set apart a portion of their home grounds for the garden. A good flower garden exerts a powerful influence upon the aesthetic side of the home life, and the vegetable garden contributes to the family's health and economy. An area of land cultivated as a kitchen garden will easily supply the family table with one hundred dollars worth of vegetables every year.

Best for the lady who tends the garden, though, is that life-giving something in the very smell of the ground, especially in the soft springtime. And when the long summer days come, when the lady drops her endless sewing and gathers what she has grown in anticipation of preparing a fresh meal—a vase of colorful blooms upon the table to meet the family when they sit—she will come back with lighter step and rosy cheeks. This is not romance, but sound common sense.

START SMALL. Most women have their time quite fully occupied with the supervision of household matters. They would like to have some flowers, because a certain amount of work among them is refreshing—really a resting spell because of its change from the monotony of work indoors. The cultivation of a small garden will not involve more labor than they can perform in odd spells, but if they attempt too much, the flowers, if they would grow them well, will call for so much attention that the idea of rest and recreation is destroyed and they will fail to enjoy the garden. Begin cautiously, and enlarge the field of operation as you feel justified in doing so.

PREPARE SOIL CAREFULLY. To prepare earth for seeds or small plants or to fill pots or window boxes, mix one part by bulk of well-rotted manure, two parts of good garden loam, and one part of sharp fine sand. Choose for this purpose manure which has been thoroughly rotted but not exposed to leaching from the weather. Mix all together in a heap, stir well with the shovel, sift, and place in boxes or in the bed prepared for the seed. If convenient, bake the soil for an hour in a hot oven. This will kill all weed seed and spores of fungus disease.

PROTECT PLANTS FROM THE WEATHER. To protect small plants from heat in hot climates, drive stakes into the ground slanting toward the north and lean boards against them so as to shade the rows. Or use light frames on lath or wooden slate and cover them with cotton cloth. To protect crops planted in winter from cold and give an early start in the spring, set the stakes slanting to the south and lean boards against them on the north side. Or cover with a mulch of ma-

---

Adorn the Garden

Among the many objects used for adornment, there is a very pretty one which we would like to see more frequently employed, and which when properly placed by the side of some walk well retired from other objects, is in itself highly suggestive. We refer to the sundial. What thoughts this monitor suggests to the mind! How silent, yet how eloquent! His must be a vacant mind indeed who can pass such a teacher without finding thought to accompany his walk. A shadow teacheth us, and we learn in the end that we have pursued but shadows.

—Woodward's *Architecture and Rural Art,* 1867

nure, straw, or leaves. But take care that this is not so thick as to keep the air from the plants, and also see that it is free from injurious weeds.

Choose old seed dealers. If you send to the florist for seed—and it is always advisable to do that, for he makes a specialty of seed growing and knows how to produce the best—be sure to patronize a reliable dealer. There are always men in all kinds of business who are not to be trusted. The old seed farms are all reliable, I think. The fact of their continuance in business proves that; for if they were not, they would, after a little, lose customers and give up.

Form a seed club. The packages of seeds put up by most seed growers generally contain more than one person will care to use. It is a good plan to club together in a country neighborhood. The cost will be less, and there will be seeds enough to divide among half a dozen persons.

A Famous Abode

Wayside, the home of the [Nathaniel] Hawthorne in Concord, was a comfortable little house on a shady, grassy road. To please his wife he had built an addition to it, a tower into which he could climb, locking out the world below, and underneath, a little parlor, in whose dainty new furnishings Mrs. Hawthorne took a womanish delight. Yet, somehow, gay Brussels rugs and gilded frames were not the background for the morbid, silent recluse.

Mrs. Hawthorne, however, made few such mistakes. She was a soft, affectionate, feminine little woman, with intuitions subtle enough to follow her husband into his darkest moods, but with, too, a cheerful, practical Yankee "capacity" which fitted her to meet baker and butcher. Nobody could have been better fitted to stand between Hawthorne and the world. She did it effectively.

— Rebecca Harding Davis, *Bits of Gossip*, 1904

Chapter Three

———•———

Principles and Practices for Keeping Servants

Domestic service, beyond doubt, constitutes the most difficult element of a well-regulated household.

The Chief Servants and Their Roles

Duties of the Housekeeper

Understand what it is you expect of your help and make clear to them your expectations.

Know what a housekeeper should be:

⚜ Necessarily she is well bred and well educated.

⚜ To her duties she often brings a knowledge of refined housekeeping gained in her own home, a knowledge of life and its conventions, and a tact to direct those serving her that is commonly given alone to those bred in early years in gentle living.

⚜ She should be possessed of thorough executive ability. She is, under the mistress, head of the house and thus hires and discharges all servants and sees personally that all work is thoroughly and properly done.

- She is, with constant kindness in her heart for human frailty, on the watch to detect and correct any wrongdoing on the part of any servant.

- She should never spy, and never go quietly to detect errors.

- Her approach should always be known.

- She should gain the good will and affection of those she directs by unfailing good order and kindly interest in each of them. If she has the confidence and respect of those under her, she has their support.

- She should have few rules, but those few most effectively kept.

- The heads of the house must fully endorse her in every detail of her administration.

THE HOUSEKEEPER'S DAY IS FULL AND COMMONLY PROCEEDS WITH THESE DUTIES:

Oversight of staff. She is up early in the morning and sees that all under her charge are at work by 7 a.m. She has planned the daily work of the other servants and must see that her directions are carried out with clock-like regularity.

Review of the pantry. After breakfast, the housekeeper goes to the pantry to see what is wanted in the way of supplies. If glass or china has been broken, it should be reported to her at once. It is well for the housekeeper to look through all drawers and closets in the pantry and also into the icebox, to see that all things are kept clean and that no stale fruit or food is by chance left behind. If servants see that the housekeeper is interested in keeping all such places in order, they themselves are more neat and careful.

Shopping. In smaller establishments, the housekeeper now makes up her lists for the grocer and her menus for lunch and dinner. When these have been examined by the mistress of the house, she goes to market and sends in all that is necessary for the day's meals. She then returns home to see that what she has ordered has been sent.

Review of house. The same duty and the unswerving vigilance with which she began the day lead her to go through all rooms of the house, to be sure that her aides have done their work properly. She sees that the bathrooms are in perfect order, the bathtubs clean, soap-dishes and racks wiped, glasses on the basin in order, and all water-closets scoured and flushed.

Care of linens. After luncheon, there is often at times a little mending needful in the table linen, and this mending sometimes falls to the housekeeper. It should be done before sending away to the laundry. A linen book is well kept in the pantry. In this book, the pantry maid should make a list of all table linen before it is sent to the wash. This linen, as well as all other soiled linen, should be taken to the laundry Friday after-

Housekeepers Oversee a Home's Laundry

noons, so that the laundress may sort it for washing Saturday. The housekeeper checks off the linen when it comes from the laundry and directs the putting away of it. The housekeeper has charge of the linen closet and sees that the supply is increased when necessary.

Ordering supplies. It is she also in many houses who gives out the daily supply of linen, orders the flowers, and sees that they are properly arranged by the butler. In fact, she often gives the butler a helping hand with the flowers, especially when no parlor maid is kept and the butler and second man have charge of the parlors. The housekeeper orders all coal, wood, etc., and in some houses she has entire charge of the wine closet, giving out daily to the butler the wines he requires and handing to the mistress a weekly list of the contents of the wine closet.

Keeping of accounts. In the evening, the housekeeper usually makes up the accounts and goes over the books of the different tradespeople, for she pays all bills and sees that in items and as a whole they are correct.

A HOUSEKEEPER TENDS TO BOTH FAMILY HOMES. If the family has a summer home, the housekeeper oversees the closing of the town house and the opening of the country house, ensuring that:

- All carpets are sent to be cleaned.
- All blankets are put away in good order.
- Heavy curtains are taken down.
- The furniture slip-covers are put on early in May.
- The lace curtains are sent to the cleaner's.
- The need of all repairs is reported to the mistress.

Duties of the Butler

In some homes, a waitress assumes many of the butler's responsibilities.

THE BUTLER HAS ENTIRE CHARGE OF THE DINING ROOM AND PANTRY. THEREBY, HE:

- Cools and warms the wines, which are usually bought by the master of the house.
- Serves the principal dishes at the table.
- Serves any refreshment required in the evening, carrying coffee to the parlor or library after dinner.
- Closes for the night all rooms under his care, and sits up awaiting the return of any members of the family who have been at the theatre, etc., and may require refreshments on their return.

THE BUTLER ALSO IS IN CHARGE OF:

- The silver, flowers, and fruits.
- The valeting of the master and sometimes of guests.

DRESS HIM SUITABLY. In the evening he wears all black, with a low-cut waistcoat that may be white if he chooses, and a white tie. At dinner, he always stands behind his master's chair.

Duties of the Useful Man

SOME HOMES HAVE IN THEIR EMPLOY "A USEFUL MAN," WHO PERFORMS THESE JOBS:

- He carries all coal and wood to kitchen and laundry and to boxes on each floor, which he keeps full.
- He carries down ashes, carries up and down all trunks and baggage, opens all express and freight packages, keeps basement, hall, trunk room, cellar, and court in order.
- He washes garbage cans and windows, cleans brasses of the house, and sweeps walk, piazza, and vestibules.
- He washes steps and sidewalk at least twice a week with the hose, shakes doormats, helps sweep bedrooms when such are very large and the furniture heavy.
- He carries all hampers of clothes to the laundry, and carries clean clothes upstairs. He freezes ice cream and attends the furnace.

Standards for the Mistress and Her Employees

Guidelines for Household Employers

A truly polite mistress will find no trouble in having good servants, for she will remember that they are human, and not stone, with feelings and rights that should be respected.

CONSIDER THESE HELPFUL RULES FOR BEING A RESPECTED MISTRESS:

- *Do* respect the feelings and attachments of your servants. Let the lovely parlor maid have her lover openly; she will have him anyway, and if you have her confidence, you may save her life-long misery.

- *Do* see that each person in your employ, especially when kept busy late in the evening, has time in the day, say an hour or two, when he or she may be alone, rest, or do what he or she wishes.

- *Do,* in arranging a changing off of work—for instance, the change about of parlor maid with waitress when one takes some hours off—see that each one clearly understands her duties and privileges. This will save misunderstanding and perhaps a complete upsetting of the domestic order.

- *Don't* give an order and then forget it and contradict yourself.

- *Don't* send orders to one servant via another if you can avoid it.

- *Don't* discuss servants in general, or those of any particular nationality, while you are being waited on at table.

- *Don't* promise a holiday, or any pleasure, and then take it back.

- *Don't* spy upon your servants; take pains to be sure they are honest and then trust them rationally.

- *Don't* expose them to temptation by leaving money carelessly about, as if it had no value for you.

- *Don't* go into your servants' rooms, unless you have reason to think they are not clean; they have a right to some privacy.

- *Don't* blame servants for every fault and then leave good service unthanked. They would rather, being human, be scolded and praised than have uniform excellence taken for granted.

- *Don't* expect in your servants a perfection which would be impossible in any human being.

- *Don't* talk of one servant in the hearing of another. Don't discuss one servant with another.

- *Don't* rely on information given you by one servant of the other without first investigating. Often, ill feeling and jealousy will prompt a false report.

- *Don't* allow the cook to stint the table of the servants. They should be well fed. It pays to drop into the kitchen at meal time and see if their meals are properly cooked and served.

- *Don't* fail to see that their beds are good and their rooms properly cared for. Give each one a separate room when it is possible.

- *Don't* expect servants to perform duties without proper utensils to use. Have dust sheets, cloths, brooms, brushes, pails, and dusters; require each servant to look after his or her own articles.

- *Don't* expect a servant to do that which you cannot do, or, if necessary, will not learn to do yourself.

- *Don't* neglect to have inventory of china, glass, silver, and bric-a-brac and of each servant's coming and going. Without this, it is difficult to keep track of various articles.

- *Don't* forget the old proverb, which has generations of human experience in it: "Like mistress like maid; like master like man."

Guidelines for Household Employees

Know what it is to be a good servant, in order to be a better employer.

A SERVANT SHOULD:

In his or her first interview, tell what he or she expects as a part of his or her place—to help and not to hinder him in the performance of his duties.

◀ Be downstairs not later than 6:30 a.m., and when there is work especially demanding an early hour, even earlier.

◀ Have any work that takes him or her in the presence or sight of the family or its guests done in the early part of the day in order not to be an annoyance or interruption to the family. (In well-organized households, servants are not in evidence after lunch except in direct personal service.)

◀ Give the employer proper notice before leaving. If servant is employed by the month, at least one week's notice is necessary, and if by the week, not less than two or three days' notice.

DO'S FOR THE COOK ABOUT KITCHEN WORK:

→ *Do* clean up as you go.

→ *Do* take care not to scatter in the kitchen.

→ *Do* be sure to put scalding water in each saucepan or stewpan as you finish using it.

→ *Do* keep your spice box always replenished, and take care to let your mistress know if you are out of anything likely to be required, that its place may at once be supplied.

→ *Do* take care of your copper utensils that the tin does not become worn off. If so, have them instantly replaced.

→ *Do* dry your saucepans before you put them away.

→ *Do* hang pudding bags and jelly cloths directly after use, air them well before you put them away so they won't smell musty, and keep them in a warm, dry place.

→ *Do* scald out the sink and sink brush after washing up your dishes and cleaning the dishpan.

→ *Do* be careful not to throw anything but water down the sink, lest you should clog it up.

→ *Do* use soap, very hot water, and clean dry towels so that you will never have sticky, greasy plates and dishes. Do change the water often. Perfectly clean plates and dishes are one proof of the cook being a good servant.

- ← *Do* be particular in washing vegetables. Lay cauliflower and cabbage in salt and water for an hour or more to get out the insects.
- ← *Do* ask for the bill of fare and get ready all you can on the day before a dinner party, to ease worry and hurry on the day.
- ← *Do* take notice of all orders that require time in the preparation of a dinner and hurry nothing.
- ← *Do* be careful of fuel. It is a great recommendation to a cook to use only the necessary amount of coal.
- ← *Do* wear plain cotton dresses and large aprons.
- ← *Do* be sure to keep your hair neat and smooth.
- ← *Do* have an eye to the interests of your mistress, not permitting waste of any kind. A cook who is just and honest and does as she would be done by is worthy of the greatest respect and may be sure of being successful and happy.

DON'TS FOR ANY SERVANT:

- ※ *Don't* decide the minute you enter a new situation that it doesn't suit you.
- ※ *Don't* regard as trustworthy any gossip that may be told you. Wait and see for yourself.
- ※ *Don't* tell an untruth about your wages. Tell what amount you have received a month when asked by an employer. Falsehood will place you in a very bad position. It is sure to be found out.
- ※ *Don't* be foolish in regard to wearing a cap. It is a great improvement to one's appearance and is worn by all first-class servants.
- ※ *Don't* listen while you are waiting at table; you will probably get things twisted and be tempted to repeat them so.
- ※ *Don't* be always standing on your dignity as to what is and is not "your place." If you cannot get along, go away. But while you are in a house, be pleasant.
- ※ *Don't* hide breakage from your mistress; it will get you into more trouble in the end than if you acknowledge the accident at once.

- *Don't* think your mistress is unbearable because she may sometimes be a little short in her manner; ladies often have worries and responsibilities of which servants have no idea.
- *Don't* spend your time comparing the ways of one mistress with those of another; each one has a right to her own rules in her own house.
- *Don't* spy on your masters and mistresses; the fact that their bread is in your mouth should be a reason for keeping it shut.
- *Don't* go through your work mechanically; try to notice how people leave things themselves and put them in that order.
- *Don't* "arrange" the papers on a desk or writing table unless expressly told to; pick them up, dust them and, where they have lain, put them down in the same place.
- *Don't* be restless and want to move too often; the longer you stay in one place, the more likely you are to get a good wedding present or legacy.
- *Don't* be influenced by friends to leave your employ without notice; to do so is an injustice to yourself as well as to your employer. If you hear of another situation and, without your employer's consent, leave at once or on the following day, you will forfeit claim to wages of your month.
- *Don't*, when September comes, be influenced by city friends and give up a good home on account of your employer's remaining in the country until October or November. Girls often do this, and it is a great mistake. They are apt to remain idle two or three weeks and then are often compelled again to go out of town and amongst strangers.
- *Don't* leave garbage in the pantry from one meal to another. Always keep the sink and pantry clean.
- *Don't* upset the cook by telling her what the family says about her cooking. Leave that for the mistress. If there is any fault to be found, it is not so apt to cause trouble if it goes direct to the cook from her mistress.

✳ *Don't* forget, when meats, turkey, and game are served, that sauce or gravy and also the jelly, such as cranberry jelly, should be served before the vegetables.

✳ *Don't* wash up while meals are being served. The noise is liable to be heard, and it is very annoying. Everything should be run quietly in dining room and pantry during meal hours.

✳ *Don't*, when you are cleaning rooms, forget your dusters and broom. Look around before you leave the room and take them with you. It is not pleasant to trip over such things.

✳ *Don't* forget to clean the finger marks from paint when you are cleaning rooms.

PART THREE

The Mistress of the Kitchen:

GENERAL GUIDELINES
FOR MEAL PREPARATION

CHAPTER ONE

——◆——

SETTING YOURSELF TO THE TASK

Method, skill, and economy in the kitchen may safely be styled the root, the foundation, of housewifery .

Learning the Essentials

We may as well start from the right point, if we hope to continue, friends. You must learn the rudiments of the art for yourself. Practice, and practice alone, will teach you certain essentials.

LEARN TO COOK NO MATTER YOUR CIRCUMSTANCES. For those who will only oversee the cooking, teach yourselves, nevertheless. As one wife relayed,: "When I took possession of my first real home, the prettily furnished cottage to which I came as a bride, more full of hope and courage than if I had been wiser, five good friends presented me with as many cookbooks, each complete and all by different compilers. One day's investigation of my menage convinced me that my lately hired servants either knew no more about cookery than I did or affected stupidity to develop my capabilities or ignorance."

The Family Meal

The soft gleam of polished silver set against fine white linen, dishes of a pattern familiar and cherished, a low glass bowl for the center of the table holding flowers in a colorful mass—you would make the setting worthy of the importance of the family meal. Dear ones gather around the family board, the day's events pass in relief, young bodies store up heat and energy for working, playing, growing. It is enough to take your breath away, this job of feeding and looking after a family, this responsibility that is yours.

—*"Kook Kwick" Pressure Cooker Recipes*, ca. 1910

REMEMBER CLEANLINESS. The last thing you should do before beginning to cook is to wash your hands and clean your nails.

SAVE FAILURES FOR YOURSELF. Scorched soups and custards, sour bread, biscuit yellow with soda, and cake heavy as lead come under the head of "hopeless." They are absolutely unfit to be set before civilized beings and educated stomachs. Should such mishaps occur, lock the memory of the attempt in your own bosom, and do not vex or amuse your guests with the narration—still less with visible proof of the calamity.

LEARN TO MANAGE A FIRE. In the first place, you need to know how to manage a fire, for if you fail in that you will fail in your cooking. Therefore, you must understand all about the dampers, and in buying a stove one should learn at the shop how and when to open and close them. When you start your fire, the dampers should all be open. Do not lay paper flat in the fire basket, but twist it in bunches, putting in first the paper, then kindlings, so crossed as to let the air draw through, placing the heavier pieces of wood upon the top. As soon as *all* are burning well, add two or three shovelfuls of coal. It is better to feed the fire often at first, but by the time you are ready to cook it must be a solid fire.

PLEASE THE PALATE BY PLEASING THE EYE. The recommendation of the eye to the palate is a point no cook can afford to disregard. A table well set is half spread. Should your cupboard be bare of aught more substantial than crackers and cheese, do not yield to dismay: split the crackers, toast the inside lightly and butter while hot, grate your cheese into a powdery mound, and garnish the edges of the plate. If you have no beverage except water to set before an unexpected visitor, let this be cool and pour it out for him yourself into an irreproachable glass.

Advice on Using Recipes

LEARN BY DOING. I'll not forget the advice of a dear friend who lifted me up from despondency when I was early married. "Bless your innocent little heart!" she cried, in her fresh, gay voice. "Ninety-nine out of a hundred cook books are written by people who never kept house, and the hundredth by a good cook who yet doesn't know how to express herself to the enlightenment of others. Compile a recipe book for yourself. Make haste slowly. Learn one thing at a time, and when you have mastered it, make a note of it, never losing sight of the principle that *you must do it in order to learn how.*"

CONSERVE TIME AND STRENGTH. Study method and economy of time no less than of materials. Before undertaking the preparation of any dish, read over the recipe carefully, unless you are thoroughly familiar with the manufacture of it. Many excellent housewives have a fashion of saying loftily, when asked how such things are made, "I carry all my recipes in my head. I never wrote out one in my life." Whereas the truth is that if you have a mind worthy of the name, its powers are too valuable to be laden with such details.

TAKE LIBERTIES WITH RECIPES. I have not said one-tenth of that which is pressing upon my heart and mind, yet I fear you may think me trite and tedious. One suggestion more, and we will proceed to the details of business. I believe that, so far as care can avail in securing such a result, my recipes are accurate. But in the matter of seasoning and other minor details, consult your judgment and your husband's taste. Take this liberty with whatever recipe you think you can improve.

Chapter Two

———•———

Cooking Terms and Measurements

Terms

One reason why there is so much uncertainty about American cookery is because many housekeepers modify a standard dish according to their own ideas and then retain the original name. If they have the ability to improve upon an accepted method, they ought to name their dish so as to give it individuality, as justly as inventors who improve upon a patent announce the changes by a new name. Thus we offer proper definitions of culinary terms.

INGREDIENTS, DISHES, AND PROCEDURES:

- *A la Creole.* Cooked with tomatoes, onions and peppers.
- *Arrowroot.* A nutritious starch obtained from a tropical American plant.
- *A la Printanière.* A soup or stew served with spring vegetables.
- *Aspic.* A savory jelly for meats, fish, vegetables and salads. Frequently used as a garnish.
- *Au Gratin.* Cooked with browned crumbs and usually with grated cheese.

Bain-marie

- ❧ *Bain-marie.* A vessel containing hot water in which other vessels containing foods are placed to keep hot without further cooking. Literally a double boiler on a large scale.

- ❧ *Bechamel.* A rich white sauce made with stock, milk, or cream.

- ❧ *Bennie.* An East Indian plant, widely cultivated for its seed (similar to sesame seed).

- ❧ *Barding.* Fastening over the breast of a bird of any kind a large thin slice of fat salt pork, which in cooking serves the purpose of basting.

- ❧ *Bisque.* A thick white sauce or soup generally made from shellfish.

- ❧ *Blanch.* To whiten by scalding.

- ❧ *Bouillon.* A meat broth.

- ❧ *Bombe.* Molded ices having the outside one variety and the center another.

- ❧ *Bouquet of Herbs.* A bunch of various flavoring herbs, used for soups or stews.

- ❧ *Braise.* To cook in a closely covered stewpan with vegetables, having a gentle heat, that neither flavor nor juices are lost by evaporation.

- ❧ *Canapé.* A finger strip of bread or toast spread with a savory compound, usually either fish or egg, daintily garnished and served as an appetizer before lunch or dinner.

- *Caper.* The greenish flower buds and young berries of the caper, which are pickled and used in sauces.
- *Chervil.* An aromatic herb of the carrot family with divided leaves, for soups and salads.
- *Claret.* Any red table wine of the Bordeaux region of France.
- *Collops.* A slice or morsel of meat for stewing; a small portion of anything.
- *Compote.* A dish of fruits cooked in syrup.
- *Croustades.* Small pieces of bread fried or toasted. Used as a garnish for minced or hashed meat.
- *Drachm.* A dram.
- *En Brochette.* Small portions of meal, such as chicken livers, cooked with bacon on a skewer.
- *Entrée.* A savory made dish served as a course itself, or between heavier courses, at dinner.
- *Eschalots.* Shallot (an onion-like vegetable).
- *Farci.* Stuffed.
- *Fondue.* Cheese and eggs cooked together.
- *Force-meat.* Finely chopped, highly seasoned meat, served separately or used as a stuffing.
- *Frappé.* Half frozen.
- *Gilding.* Gilding is covering any surface of food with the yolk of a raw egg and subsequently drying or browning it in the oven. Fancy pastry is generally gilded.
- *Glacé.* Glazed over. In savory dishes with meat stock, boiled down to a glaze; in sweet cookery, iced or brushed over with white of egg.
- *Gridiron.* A grated utensil for broiling.
- *Grist.* Ground corn.
- *Ground nut.* The peanut.
- *Hommony.* Maize, hulled and broken, to be boiled for food.

- ❧ *Hors d'œuvres.* Small dishes served during the first course of a dinner.
- ❧ *Hyson tea.* A green tea from China having a special twist.
- ❧ *Isinglass.* Gelatin made from bladders of certain fishes.
- ❧ *Jardinière.* Mixed vegetables.
- ❧ *Lard.* To insert strips of fat pork or bacon in meats deficient in fat, with a larding needle.
- ❧ *Leek.* A culinary herb of the lily family, allied to the onion.
- ❧ *Macédoine.* A mixture of vegetables or fruits.
- ❧ *Marinate.* To make savory in a mixture of seasonings, often oil and vinegar or oil and lemon juice.
- ❧ *Meringue.* White of egg and sugar beaten together.
- ❧ *Mousse.* May be savory or sweet. A light, frothy mixture thickened with gelatin with a whisk till spongy in texture and then packed in ice and salt for three or four hours.
- ❧ *Mulligatawny.* A rich soup flavored with curry.
- ❧ *N. B.* Nata bene (note well).
- ❧ *Orgeat.* A flavoring syrup prepared with an emulsion of almonds.
- ❧ *Pap.* A soft food for infants.
- ❧ *Pâté.* A small pastry shell, usually made from puff paste. May contain either a sweet or savory filling.
- ❧ *Piggin.* A small wooden vessel having one stave projecting above the rim for the handle.
- ❧ *Purée.* Meats, vegetables, fish, etc., cooked in liquid till tender, then passed through a sieve.
- ❧ *Rasher.* A thin slice of meat.
- ❧ *Ratafia.* Any liqueur flavored with fruit kernels, especially of a bitter almond flavor.
- ❧ *Roux.* A cooked mixture of butter and flour for thickening soups, sauces and gravies.

- *Rusk.* A light, sweetened bread or biscuit; bread or cake that has been crisped and browned in the oven, then often pounded fine to be eaten with milk.

- *Saffron.* A deep orange color, from an autumn flowering species of crocus plant.

- *Sago.* A starch prepared from the pith of an East Indian or Malaysian palm (sago palm), used in puddings and to stiffen textiles.

- *Salaeratus.* Baking soda.

- *Salamander.* Many of various articles used in connection with the fire, as in the culinary utensil for browning pastry.

- *Salmi.* A rich stew of game, half roasted and then cut up and cooked in a sauce.

- *Salsify.* A European biennial herb of the chicory family, with a long spindle-shaped edible root.

- *Saltpeter.* Mineral salt consisting of mitric acid and potassium, used in making gunpowder and in curing meat.

- *Sauté.* To cook till brown in a shallow pan with a little fat.

- *Scrag.* The nape of the neck, especially in sheep.

- *Shaddock.* A pear-shaped citrus fruit resembling the grapefruit, but having coarse dry flesh of poor quality.

- *Shallots.* An onion-like culinary vegetable, allied to garlic but having milder bulbs, used for seasoning and pickles.

- *Sippets.* Toasted or fried bread for garnishing.

- *Sorrel.* Herb with acid leaves.

- *Soufflé.* Puffed up and made light by use of well-beaten eggs. May be savory or sweet.

- *Spider.* A metal pan with a handle, used in frying food. Originally it had long legs for use over coals.

- *Suet.* The fatty tissue about the loins and kidneys of sheep, oxen, etc. Used in cookery and for making tallow.

- ❧ *Sweet-bread.* The thymus or pancreas of an animal, used for food, the thymus, being sweet-bread or throat sweet-bread, the pancreas being stomach sweet-bread.
- ❧ *Syllabub.* A dish made by mixing wine or cider with milk, forming a soft curd.
- ❧ *Tallow.* Animal fat.
- ❧ *Tartaric acid.* A substitute for lemon juice.
- ❧ *Terrapin.* Turtle or tortoise, living in fresh or brackish water, highly valued as food.
- ❧ *Truffle.* Eatable mushroom, growing underground.
- ❧ *Truss.* To fasten as with skewers or twine, as a fowl before cooking.
- ❧ *Tureen.* A deep vessel for soup, etc.
- ❧ *Turmeric.* The root of an East Indian plant of the ginger family, used as a condiment.
- ❧ *Vermicelli.* Wheat paste, made into worm-like strands.
- ❧ *Vol-au-vent.* A very light case of puff paste in which savories or sweets may be served.

Measures

HOUSEHOLD MEASURES FOR SOLID INGREDIENTS INCLUDE:

Wheat flour	1 pound is 1 quart.
Indian meal	1 pound 2 ounces are 1 quart.
Butter	When soft, 1 pound is 1 pint.
Loaf sugar	Broken, 1 pound is 1 quart.
Powdered white sugar	1 pound 1 ounce are 1 quart.
Best brown sugar	1 pound 2 ounces are 1 quart.
Eggs	10 eggs are 1 pound.
Flour	8 quarts are 1 peck; 4 pecks are 1 bushel.

HOUSEHOLD MEASURES FOR LIQUID INGREDIENTS INCLUDE:

- ❋ 1 tablespoonful is ½ ounce.
- ❋ 60 drops are equal to 1 teaspoonful.
- ❋ 4 teaspoonfuls. are equal to 1 tablespoonful.
- ❋ 16 large tablespoonfuls are ½ pint.
- ❋ 8 large tablespoonfuls are 1 gill.
- ❋ 2 gills are ½ pint.
- ❋ A common sized tumbler holds ½ pint.

THE BEST COOK'S MEASURE FOR DONENESS IS AMBER:

- ❋ Keep covered everything that is being fried. Doing this will enable you to fry articles of food *a pretty amber color,* while at the same time it will be perfectly done.

- ❋ For example, when frying chicken, cover closely and fry *till a fine amber color.* When roasting turkey, baste and turn frequently *till every part is a beautiful brown amber color.*

- ❋ In baking bread, *when the top of the loaf is a light amber color,* put back the paper that the bread may not brown too much while thoroughly baking.

- ❋ The *palest amber jelly,* clear and sparkling, flavored only by the grated rind and juice of a lemon and pale Madeira or sherry wine, is not only the most beautiful, but the most palatable jelly that can be made.

- ❋ When making tomato preserves, take the boiled tomatoes out *when they become amber colored.* In making peach preserves, when all the peaches have been boiled and set in the sun, put back the first dish of peaches in the kettle, *taking them out when a pretty amber color,* and so on till all have been boiled twice.

Chapter Three

———◆———

$\mathcal{P}$REPARING COMMON FOODS

Herein, rather than giving recipes for specific dishes—those come later—I have imparted bits of wisdom earned with experience regarding the general preparation of the foods we most often consume. These are matters often taken for granted by cooks of some years and left out of so many named recipes. These thoughts follow no particular system; they are simply notable observations made during my life.

Foods for Every Meal

$\mathcal{B}$read

"When the bread rises in the oven, the heart of the housewife rises with it." The speaker of this truth might have added that the heart of the housewife sinks in sympathy with sinking bread. Bread is so vitally important in our nourishment that I have assigned it the first place here.

BE NOT DAUNTED. I would recommend that the housekeeper acquire the practice as well as the theory of bread-making. If circumstances should throw her out of a cook for a short time, she is then prepared for the emergency. In this country, fortunes are so rapidly made and lost, the vicissitudes of life are so sudden, that we know not what a day may bring forth. On the other hand, there is no reason why the food of the poor should not be as well prepared and palatable as that of the wealthy. For, by care and pains, the finest bread may be made of the simplest materials, and surely the loving hands of the poor man's wife and daughter will take as much pains to make his bread nice and light as hirelings will do for the wealthy.

USE GOOD FLOUR. Good flour is an indispensable requisite to good bread and, next, good yeast and sufficient kneading. Only experience will enable you to be a good judge of flour. One test is to rub the dry flour between your fingers, and if the grains feel round, it is a sign that the flour is good. If after trying a barrel of flour twice, you find it becomes wet and sticky after being made up to the proper consistency, you had better then return it to your grocer.

USE GOOD YEAST. The best flour is worthless without good yeast. Yeast should be foamy and frothy with a scent slightly like ammonia.

SUN AND AIR FLOUR BEFORE USE. In the morning, get out the flour to be made up at night for next morning's breakfast. Sift it in a tray and put it out in the sun, or, if the day is damp, set it near the kitchen fire.

LEARN THE ART OF MIXING. There is a great art in mixing bread, and it is necessary to observe a certain rotation in the process. To make a small quantity of bread: first sift one quart of flour; into that sift a teaspoonful of salt; next rub in an Irish potato, boiled and mashed fine; then add a piece of lard the size of a walnut; and next a half teacup of yeast in which three teaspoonfuls of white sugar have been stirred. Then make into a soft dough with lukewarm water or milk. If the water with which you mix your dough is too hot, it will kill the yeast. Milk should be scalded and then allowed to cool, as the acid in unscalded milk may sour the bread.

KNEAD STEADILY. Knead without intermission for at least half an hour, *by the clock*. When none of the dough sticks to your hands, you can leave off kneading, but not until then, as rested dough is not nearly so nice. Then place it in a stone crock, greased with lard at the bottom, and set it to rise.

PLAN AROUND RISING TIME. As bread rises much more quickly in summer than in winter; you must make allowance for this difference during the respective seasons. The whole process, including both the first and second rising, may be accomplished in seven or eight hours in summer—though this will be regulated partly by the flour, as some kinds of flour rise much more quickly than others. For breakfast, you may make it up at 9 o'clock p.m. in summer for an 8 o'clock breakfast next morning; but in winter, make it up at 7 p.m. If hot bread is desired for dinner, reserve part of the breakfast dough, keeping it in the kitchen in winter and in the icebox in summer till two hours before dinner.

SET BREAD TO RISE BY SEASON. Set bread to rise in a cool place in summer but in a warm place, free from draughts, in winter. In the latter season, the stone crock may be wrapped in a blanket or set on bread-warming shelf under which a lighted coal-oil lamp is placed.

To Make Home Happy

The most important of all things pertaining to the kitchen and cookery, to happiness and health, is the "Staff of Life," otherwise GOOD BREAD and BISCUITS, to say nothing of the thousand and one delicacies of cakes, waffles, puddings, pies, etc. that the children love so much, and which, when well made and properly cooked, are no detriment to health, but are, on the contrary, both nourishing and of the greatest value in giving variety to the somewhat monotonous routine of meat and vegetables that go to make up the bill of fare of the average American family.

—*Cow Brand Soda Cook Book and Facts Worth Knowing,* 1900

Bread or Biscuits?

It is a woeful thing that the daughters of New England have abandoned the old respectable mode of yeast brewing and bread raising for this specious substitute, so easily made, and so seldom well made. The green, clammy, acrid substance, called biscuit, which many of our worthy republicans are obliged to eat in these days, is wholly unworthy of the men and women of the Republic. Good patriots ought not to be put off in that way; they deserve better fare.

—Harriet Beecher Stowe,
House and Home Papers, 1869

SERVE BREAD PROPERLY. When thoroughly done and taken from the oven, it should be placed on its side or top crust so that the steam can get out of the bottom of the loaf, which is not so hard as the top crust. Then wrap the bread a few moments in a clean, thick bread towel and send it to the table with a napkin over it, to be kept on till each person has taken his seat at the table.

INTRODUCE VARIETY. Do not constantly make bread in the same shapes; each morning, try to have some variation. Plain light bread dough may be made into loaves, rolls, twists, turnovers, and light biscuits, and these changes of shape make a pleasant and appetizing variety in the appearance of the table. As bread is far more appetizing baked in pretty shapes, I would suggest the snowball shape for muffins and egg bread. Very pretty iron shapes (8 or 12 in a group, joined together) may be procured from almost any tinner.

TIPS ON TOASTING: If you have a large family to toast for, you can get on faster if you lay the slices on the rack in the oven to dry a little while the first pieces are being prepared. Toast can be made over a clean grate fire, but it is nicer when held before the fire. In serving dry toast, slices should not be piled one upon another, but placed edgewise; piling it makes it tough instead of crisp, as the steam cannot escape when piled.

Boston Cream Toast

As Boston claims to be the "hub" upon which the world turns, I have thought to close the toast making [discussion] with the Bostonian plan of making cream toast. It will be found very nice, and the second dish, or plan, using the same cream, will undoubtedly suit many persons—try them both…

Cut stale bread in slices one-fourth inch thick and toast a nice light chestnut color. Put 1 pint of milk to heat with ½ cup of butter, a little pepper, and salt to suit the taste. Blend 2 large teaspoons of flour with cold milk, and when it boils, stir in and let it boil 2 or 3 minutes. Now have ready a pan of hot water, a little salted, dip each slice quickly in the water, lay in a hot dish and cover with the hot cream. Serve immediately.

Another nice dish is made by rolling light bread dough thin, cutting in strips, and boiling in hot fat. Break each cake open as it comes from the kettle and plunge it into the above cream.

—A.W. Chase, *Dr. Chase's Third Last and Complete Receipt Book and Household Physician,* 1903

Milk and Butter

The most exquisite nicety and care must be observed in the management of milk and butter.

KEEP ON HAND TWO SETS OF VESSELS. A housekeeper should have two sets of milk vessels (tin or earthenware, never stoneware, as this is an absorbent). She should never use twice in succession the same milk vessels without having them scalded and aired.

SET ASIDE PLENTY. In warm weather, sweet milk should be set on ice, if practicable; or if not, in a spring house. Never put ice in sweet milk,

Good Butter

*Y*et the process of making good butter is a very simple one. To keep the cream in a perfectly pure, cool atmosphere, to churn while it is yet sweet, to work out the buttermilk thoroughly, and to add salt with such discretion as not to ruin the fine, delicate flavor of the fresh cream—all this is quite simple, so simple that one wonders at thousands and millions of pounds of butter yearly manufactured which are merely a hobgoblin—a bewitchment of cream into foul and loathsome poisons."

—Harriet Beecher Stowe,
House and Home Papers, 1869

as this dilutes it. One pan of milk should always be set aside to raise cream for coffee. One bucket with a tight lid should be filled with milk and set aside for dinner, one for supper, one for breakfast, and a fourth for cooking.

SCALD THE CHURN. A stone churn is in some respects more convenient than a wooden churn; but no matter which you use, the most fastidious neatness must be observed. Have the churn scalded and set out to sun as soon as possible after churning. Use your last made butter for buttering bread, reserving the staler for cookery.

CHURN CAREFULLY. When making butter, strain unskimmed milk into a scalded churn. This will give a sweeter butter and nicer buttermilk than when cream is skimmed and kept for churning, as this sometimes gives a cheesy taste to the butter. Do not let the milk in the churn exceed blood heat. If overheated, the butter will be white and frothy and the milk thin and sour. Churn as soon as the milk is turned. In summer, try to churn early in the morning, as fewer flies are swarming then and the butter can be made much firmer.

PRINT AND REFRIGERATE CORRECTLY. Butter should be printed early in the morning, while it is cool. A plateful for each of the three meals should be placed in the icebox ready for use. Do not set butter in a icebox with anything else in it but milk, or in a safe with anything but milk. It readily imbibes the flavor of everything near it.

Eggs

While eggs are nourishing, they are not so heating to the blood as meat, and doctors often order them for patients who need nourishment and yet cannot have their blood heated by meat juices. Even when they cost the most, you can really get more nourishment from them than for the same amount of money spent for meat.

TRY SHIRRING EGGS. This form of cooking eggs is a modification of baking them. Small earthen dishes are used, each one holding an egg; the dishes are buttered, an egg put into each one without mixing the white and yolk, and a little salt and pepper dusted over the eggs. The eggs should be covered with a buttered paper to prevent the browning of the surface. The dishes are then placed upon the back of the stove or in a moderate oven. When the whites of the eggs are set, the dishes are then sent to the table and the eggs eaten from them.

TRY VARIOUS OMELETS. There is an infinite variety of omelets, named from the special flavor or seasoning given by any predominating ingredient. The sweet light omelets are used either for breakfast or plain desserts; the plain omelets are suitable for breakfast and luncheon. In parsley and fine herbs omelets, the chopped herbs are mixed with the eggs before the omelet is cooked; grated ham, tongue, and cheese are also mixed in the same way. In many other omelets, the special ingredient used is enclosed in the omelet.

DYE EGGS FOR EASTER. Easter morning would be incomplete, for the children at least, without the brightly colored eggs typical of the day. When prepared dyes are not available, varied colors may be produced by: boiling a small quantity of the following with the eggs: for red, Brazil wood; for yellow, Persian berries or a very little tumeric; for brown, a strong dye of tumeric; for a claret color, log wood; for black, logwood and chromate of potash; for blue, a mixture of powdered indigo and crystals of sulphate or iron; for reddish-purple, red onion skins.

DECORATE EGGS FOR EASTER. An old-fashioned method was to tie each egg in a piece of figured chintz or calico, which would leave its imprint on the egg after it was exposed to the action of boiling water. To color the eggs with original designs, a provincial method was to trace figures upon the shells of raw eggs with a bit of hard tallow candle, thus covering the part of the shell which was desired white, and then to put the eggs in boiling dyed water. Sometimes the eggs are entirely dyed, and then designs are engraved upon them with a sharp knife or a strong trussing or darning needle.

Select Unblemished Eggs to Dye and Decorate

Teas

BOIL DIFFERENT TEA TYPES FOR DIFFERENT TIMES. Of all "cups that cheer," there is nothing like the smoking hot cup of tea, made with *boiling* water, in a *thoroughly scalded* tea pot. If it is the good old-fashioned green tea of "ye ancient time," you must just put it to *draw* and not to boil; if it is genuine "English Breakfast" or *best* black tea, the water must not only be boiling hot, at the very moment of pouring it on, but the tea must actually boil for at least five or ten minutes.

MAKE A TEA POT BONNET. To insure "keeping hot" while serving, make the simple contrivance known as a "bonnet" which is warranted a "sure preventive" against that most insipid of all drinks—"a warmish cup of tea." It is merely a sack with a loose elastic in the bottom large enough to cover and encircle the entire tea pot. Make it with odd pieces of silk, satin, or cashmere, lined, quilted, and embroidered, if you like. Draw this over the tea pot as soon as the tea is poured into it, and it will remain piping hot for half an hour.

Common Meats and Game

Principles for Preparing Meat

KNOW HOW LONG YOUR MEAT WILL KEEP: In average temperate weather, clear and dry, you can keep meat which has not been frozen for the following lengths of time:

- ☞ Veal and pork: one day.
- ☞ Lamb: two days.
- ☞ Beef and mutton: from three to ten days.
- ☞ Large poultry and game birds: from three to six days.
- ☞ Small game: from two to five days.
- ☞ Large game: about a week.

TRY RESTORING TAINTED MEAT. If salted, wash it, and throw away the old brine, then replace it with the following composition, and let it lie in it for a few days: freshly burnt charcoal, powdered, 12 parts; common salt, 11 parts; saltpeter, 4 parts. Mix. This must be used the same as common salt, and when you want to cook the meat, the black colour may be removed with clean water.

HEED THESE KEEPING TIMES BEFORE USING PREPARED MEATS:

🌼 Soak all *hams* 24 hours before cooking.

🌼 *Corn beef* must remain packed down in salt for ten or twelve days before being put in brine; it is fit for use after two weeks in brine.

🌼 Before hanging *beef* to smoke, it must remain for ten days in the salt, brown sugar, molasses, and saltpeter that has been rubbed on it.

🌼 *Spiced beef* must remain three to four weeks in a wooden box or tub, in which it is turned occasionally in the pickle it makes and rubbed with salt.

🌼 Allow three weeks to prepare *cured beef ham* for use. Let it remain in molasses a day and two nights and in molasses and salt for ten additional days; hang it up to dry for one week, then smoke it a little and keep hanging till used.

When the weather will admit of it, *mutton* is better for being kept a few days before cooking.

Truffle dressing is usually placed in the turkey two days beforehand to impart its flavor to the fowl. A *goose* must never be eaten the same day it is killed; if the weather is cold, it should be kept a week before using and before cooking should lie several hours in weak salt and water to remove the strong taste.

Kill *young ducks* some days before using; or, if obliged to use them the same day as killed, they are better roasted.

ROAST MEAT BEFORE AN OPEN FIRE. If possible, roast meat on a spit before a large, open fire, where there is the intense heat required for cooking and the constantly changing current of air necessary to carry away from the meat the fumes of burning fat, which impair its flavor.

BROIL AS YOU WOULD ROAST. Meat for broiling should be cut from an inch to an inch and a half thick; the surface should be scraped with the back of a knife to remove sawdust and bone dust, and then wiped with a wet cloth. While the meat is being broiled, heat a dish to receive it; after it is laid upon the hot dish, season it with salt, pepper, and butter on both sides and serve it at once. Broiled meat deteriorates if left standing near the fire any length of time after it is cooked

BAKE MEAT, IF NECESSARY, AT PROPER TEMPERATURES. Baking is not the most desirable way of cooking meat, but the ovens are often available when an open fire cannot be reached. It is desirable that the first exposure of meat should be to the greatest obtainable heat, in order to quickly crisp its surface and confine its natural juices.

KEEP MEAT FLAVORING ON HAND. As the housekeeper is sometimes hurried in preparing a dish, it will save time and trouble for her to keep on hand a bottle of meat flavoring compounded by putting in a quart bottle and covering with cider vinegar: two chopped onions, three pods of red pepper (chopped), two tablespoons brown sugar, one tablespoon each of celery seed and ground mustard, and one teaspoonful each of black pepper and salt. A tablespoonful of this mixed in a stew, steak, or gravy will impart not only a fine flavor but also a rich color.

Calf

ASK THE BUTCHER TO PREPARE IT SOMEWHAT. Have the butcher to remove the hair by scalding and scraping, to remove the teeth and the eyes from the head, and to split the head in two pieces without cutting the tongue or brains. Likewise, have him split the feet.

REMEMBER AT HOME, FOR CALF, TO:

☙ Thoroughly wash the *head* in plenty of cold water, carefully scraping the interior of the nasal passage and the mouth. Cover the *head, feet, and tongue* in cold water with a heaping tablespoonful of salt and a tablespoon of whole peppercorns or a small red pepper; boil them over the fire until the bones can be pulled out easily. Strain the broth in which the head is boiled and save for soup.

☙ Take the *tongue* up as soon as it is tender, strip the skin off, wrap the tongue in a wet cloth, and keep it in a cool place until it is wanted.

☙ Pull off all the outer membrane from between the folds of the *brain*—being careful not to break the substance of the brain—after it

☞

Coooking Stoves

*T*he introduction of cooking stoves offers to careless domestics facilities for gradually drying up meats, and despoiling them of all flavor and nutriment, facilities which appear to be very generally laid hold of. They have almost banished the genuine, old-fashioned roast meat from our tables, and left in its stead dried meats with their most precious and nutritive juices evaporated. How few cooks, unassisted, are competent to the simple process of broiling a beefsteak or mutton chop! How very generally one has to choose between these meats gradually dried away, or burned on the outside and raw within!

—Harriet Beecher Stowe,
House and Home Papers, 1869

has lain for an hour in cold water containing a handful of salt. When the brain is quite freed from the membrane, put it over the fire in enough cold water to cover it with a teaspoonful each of salt and whole peppercorns. Let it boil for ten or fifteen minutes; then cool it, wrap it in a wet cloth, and keep it in a cool place.

🎨 Wash well in plenty of cold salted water the *tripe*—the walls and fatty portions of the stomachs of calves and cows, which is nutritious and digestible, as well as cheap.

PREPARE THE BRAIN FOR SERVING. The brain may be heated in any good sauce and served as a separate dish. It may also be made into fritters or *croquettes,* or into force meat balls for garnishing the calf's head by mixing it with an equal quantity of breadcrumbs, two raw eggs, and salt and pepper, and then either frying or poaching.

PREPARE THE TRIPE FOR SERVING. It should be boiled until tender in salted water, and then scraped with the back of a knife; after that, it can be pickled in scalding hot spiced vinegar or kept in milk or buttermilk for several days. Tripe is usually broiled or fried, sometimes being first breaded or rolled in flour. It is an excellent winter food, when some of the meats most generally used are scarce and expensive. If prepared for the table after the first boiling, it requires rather high seasoning.

Pork

SELECT YOUNG PIGS FOR ROASTING. A roasting pig is in prime condition when it is three to six weeks old, with a soft, clean, pinkish-white skin, plump hams, a short curly tail, thin delicate ears, and a soft, fringe-like margin all around the tongue.

PREPARE THE PIG FOR ROASTING. As soon as it is killed, plunge it into cold water for five minutes; then rub it all over with powdered resin and put it into scalding water for one minute. Lay it on a clean board and pull and scrape off the bristles, taking care not to injure the skin. When all the bristles are removed, wash the pig thoroughly, first in warm water and then several times in plenty of cold water. Then slit the pig from the throat downward and take out the entrails, laying the heart, liver, lights, and spleen in cold salted water. Wash the pig again in cold water, and wrap it from the air with a cloth wet in cold water until it is wanted for use.

SELECT A TENDER HOG. Hogs weighing from 150 to 200 pounds are the most suitable size for family use. They should not exceed twelve months in age, as they are much more tender from being young, and should have been corn-fed for several weeks.

SALT THE HAMS. In order to impart redness to the hams, rub on each a teaspoonful of pulverized saltpeter before salting. If the weather is very cold, warm the salt before applying it. First, rub and salt the skin side well, and then the fleshy side, using for the purpose a shoe sole or leather glove. No more salt should be used than a sufficiency to preserve the meat, as an excess hardens the meat. A bushel of salt is sufficient for a thousand pounds of meat. For the chine and ribs, a very light sprinkling of salt will suffice.

Game

STUFF AND ROAST. For partridges, pheasants, quails, or grouse, carefully cut out all the shot, wash thoroughly but quickly in water and soda, rinse again, and dry with a clean cloth. Stuff them and sew them up. Skewer the legs and wings to the body, larder the breast with very thin slices of fat salt pork, place them in the oven, and baste

Roasted Game, a Favorite

with butter and water before taking up, having seasoned them with salt and pepper. You can leave out the pork and use only butter, or cook them without stuffing. Make a gravy of the drippings thickened with browned flour. Boil up and serve in a boat.

BROIL AND SERVE WITH GRAVY. These are all very fine broiled, first splitting down the back, placing on the gridiron the inside down, cover with a baking tin, and broil slowly at first. Serve with cream gravy.

Terrapin and Green Turtle

Terrapin and green turtle are distinctive enough to be made a separate course at dinner. Only the flesh, eggs, and liver are ordinarily used. Madeira is the proper wine for terrapin, and punch is served with green turtle.

DRESS IT PROPERLY.

❀ Loosen the sides of the shells of boiled terrapin, as they are cool enough to handle.

❀ Lift off the top shell, pull or cut apart the small bands of flesh which hold it to the spine of the terrapin, then rein the undershell. The entrails of the terrapin have the eggs and liver embedded in them, and the legs are attached to them by crossing bands of flesh.

❀ Pull off the legs, leaving the flesh attached to them; break off the sharp claws at the extremities of the feet. Separate and throw away the head, and put the legs on a dish.

❀ Carefully remove the eggs and put them into a bowl of hot water; separate the liver from the entrails and cut out that part of the liver which contains the small, dark green gall bag visible on one side. The utmost care should taken to avoid cutting or breaking the gall bag; in removing it, the liver should be held over an empty dish, and if the gall bag is cut or broken, the liver should be thrown away and the hands washed before the dressing of the terrapin is resumed.

❀ Cut the liver into half-inch squares and put it with the flesh of the terrapin.

Shellfish

The custom generally prevails in this country of beginning every dinner, where there is any attempt at formality, with small shellfish served on the half shell. Even in the inland towns, oysters and hard clams can usually be procured, for they are now shipped in barrels from the eastern seaboard to all parts of the country accessible by rail. The proper accompaniments for raw shellfish are lemon and brown bread with butter.

HEED THIS ADVICE FOR PREPARING OYSTERS, MUSSELS, AND LOBSTER:

✖ The newest fashion in serving raw oysters is to surround them with what is called sea moss, made of spinach, which hides the fine chopped ice in which the oysters are embedded.

✖ If the shells of mussels are at all muddy or sandy, they should be laid for an hour or longer in a tub of cold water containing a handful of salt and then thoroughly washed before they are boiled. Place mussels in a large kettle to boil with half a pint of water, and set them over the fire until the shells open; the liquor which flows from them should be carefully strained and kept to use with them. Next, take them from the shells, carefully remove all the fine filaments attached, and cut off the tip of the tongue and the dark, fringe-like edge or "beard" which surrounds the gills. The thread-like filaments or moss that attach the mussel to the rocks or wharves where it is found are thought to be poisonous and should be carefully removed after boiling and before dressing. Some cooks use a silver spoon in preparing mussels, thinking that it will become blackened if they are unfit for food.

✖ Have over the fire a large pot full of boiling water, containing a handful of salt; plunge a live lobster heavy in proportion to its size head first into the boiling water, which will kill it at once, and boil it steadily for twenty minutes or until the shell turns red. As soon as it can be handled, break off the claws and tail and carefully remove the soft fins which lie close to the body where the legs join it. An ordinary iron can opener is very useful in breaking apart the shell of the lobster. After the shell is separated so that the flesh can be reached, save all the green fat, coral, and white curd-like substance which lies close to the shell; remove all flesh from the claws and body and cut it in half-inch pieces; split the shell of the tail, remove and throw away the intestine which runs through the center of the tail; and save the flesh. The lobster will then be ready to dress for recipes.

Fish

Fish is a very healthful and digestible food. Though not nearly so nutritious as meat, it is considered by many physicians a good brain food, especially if it is broiled.

PRESERVE LIVING FISH. Stop their mouths up with crumbs of bread steeped in brandy, pour a very small quantity of brandy into them, and pack them in clean straw. In this way, it is said fish may be preserved in a torpid state for twelve or fifteen days, and when put into water will come to life again after three or four hours.

CLEAN AGAIN AT HOME. Although they should be cleaned at the market, one should not trust entirely such cleaning, but pass the edge of the knife over the fish to remove any remaining scales. Wash it inside and out with a wet cloth, and dry carefully with a towel. Rub it next with salt and pepper, and lay it on a dish or hang it up till you are ready to cook. Never keep it lying in water, either in preparing it for cooking or in trying to keep it till the next day.

PREPARE SAUCES FOR SOME. The very dry-fleshed fish should be served with a sauce. White fish have far less oil distributed through their bodies and are therefore not so rich as darker-colored fish, and need richer sauces and dressings. In making sauces for fish, never use the water in which the fish has been boiled. Larded fish is generally stuffed and served with a brown mushroom sauce.

Additional Courses

Vegetables

Every food that has grown in the ground is called a vegetable. Not until they are growing near where we live can we expect to find them cheap. During the summer, if you can get them fresh and cook them nicely, you will not need to buy nearly as much meat and can make many nice dishes, mostly all vegetables.

BOIL SEEDS LENGTHILY. Vegetables such as wheat, oats, corn, and rice all contain more starch than anything else. The skin of all these seeds cracks in the boiling water, and the inside swells and becomes gummy. Therefore, long boiling is essential for all starched foods.

BOIL OR DRY CORN. Cold-boiled corn, cut from the ear and mixed with an equal quantity of cold potatoes chopped, can be fried with salt, pepper, and butter or heated with cold stewed tomatoes and served on toast. Alternately, cut the grains from ears of tender corn, spread them on large sheets of paper in the sun, and dry them thoroughly; or put them on pans in a cool oven and dry them. After the corn is dried, keep it in a cool, dry place. When it is wanted for the table, soak it overnight in enough water or milk to cover it. The next day boil it tender in the same water; season it with salt, pepper, and butter; and serve it hot.

PRESERVE TOMATOES FOR WINTER. Take the tomatoes when perfectly ripe and scald them in hot water in order to take off the skin easily. When skinned, boil them well in a little sugar or salt but no water. Then spread them in cakes about an inch thick and place the cakes in the sun. They will, in three or four days, be sufficiently dried to pack away in bags, which should hang in a dry place.

PICK AND SOAK ROOTS. Roots, including carrots, oyster plants, beets, potatoes, and parsnips, are mostly vegetables that will last all winter if properly taken care of. Toward spring, you must pick off the sprouts, lest they become rank; soak them to plump them; and cook

Tomatoes

$\mathcal{A}$ Massachusetts gardener sells ripe tomatoes in December by sowing the seeds in July, then potting the plants in a nine-inch jar, and maturing in a greenhouse with artificial heat as soon as needed.

An infusion of tomato leaves has been recently found to not only destroy plant lice, but from its peculiar odor to prevent their return for a long time.

—A.W.Chase, *Dr. Chase's Third Last and Complete Receipt Book and Household Physician,* 1903

them with greater care. The roots are particularly nice when they first come, if quite ripe. When young and tender, they require less time to cook.

DON'T ADD COLD MILK FOR MASHING POTATOES. Mashed potatoes will be hard, sticky, and heavy if you turn cold milk upon them while they are steaming hot, but, by adding scalding milk and beating them thoroughly, they will be light and feathery. Until served, they should be covered close with a napkin.

PROCURE PLENTY OF SPINACH. In respect to quantity, spinach is desperately deceitful. I never see it drained after it is boiled without thinking of a young housekeeper of my acquaintance, who purchased a quart of spinach and ordered a spring dinner for herself and husband. When it should have appeared upon the table, there came in its stead a platter of sliced egg, she having given out one for the dressing. "Where is the spinach?" she demanded of the maid of all work. "Under the egg, ma'am!" And it was really all there. The moral: get enough spinach to be visible to the naked eye. A peck is not too much for a family of four or five.

USE SALT FOR SOME, SUGAR FOR OTHERS. Asparagus and celery are both cooked as a vegetable and seasoned with butter and salt, but rhubarb, which is more for a sauce, has only sugar cooked in it.

Onions per Acre

In answer to an inquiry of a correspondent who asked: "How many onions can be raised to the acre," the editor of the *Congregationalist,* of Boston, responds: "In answer to the above, we give a letter received recently from Deer Island, Boston Harbor, where one of the public institutions of Boston is located. 'In reply to yours of this date, I would say that in the year 1869, we raised, on 7 acres of land, 5,000 bushels of onions, good measure. I selected and had measured off one-half an acre of land where the crop was the best, and measured from this one-half acre 486 bushels of onions. The onions grew very large. I sent 1 bushel to the fair that averaged 1 pound each.'"

—A.W. Chase, *Dr. Chase's Third Last and Complete Receipt Book and Household Physician,* 1903

Soup

Most Americans, rich and poor, have some kind of soup every day, either for an entire meal or for a first course of a dinner. As making soup is a tedious process, it is best to make enough at once to last several days.

USE UNCOOKED MEAT FOR CLEAR SOUPS. Meat and bones should be washed thoroughly, but quickly, in hot water before being put on the fire in cold water. Allow one pound of meat and bone to one quart of water in making stock; be particular to keep closely covered, but skim carefully the first part of the cooking. A cup of cold water poured in will make the scum rise freely.

ALWAYS KEEP MEAT WATER. Never throw away water in which any sort of meat has been boiled, as it much better to simmer hash or a stew in this liquor than in water, and it is also invaluable for basting fowls or meats that have not been parboiled. Strain and season just enough for one meal, reserving the rest as foundation for another sort of soup.

Macaroni and Spaghetti

Good Italian macaroni, both large and small, can now be bought in nearly all American cities.

PREPARE PROPERLY. Macaroni should never be washed before boiling; if it is dusty, wipe it with a dry cloth. Put it over the fire in plenty of salted boiling water and boil it fast for ten minutes or until it is just tender. Then drain it and throw it into cold water; this washing will remove the excess of farinaceous matter that makes it sticky. After cooling in the cold water, it can be heated in any sauce preferred, and the kind of sauce used will give the name to the dish. Tomato, mushroom, and white sauces are usually employed.

ADD MEAT TO THE DISH. The addition of a little chopped cold ham, tongue, or chicken to macaroni makes a delicious dish; as does the addition of white and tomato sauce and some chopped mushrooms and meat or poultry. Fried onions are very good with macaroni, making the favorite Italian farmer's dish.

ADD CHEESE AND BAKE. Boiled macaroni layered with grated cheese and moistened with white sauce or a little milk and butter makes a good baked dish; a few bread crumbs may be put over the top.

USE AS A GARNISH. Macaroni or spaghetti dressed with a little mushroom sauce makes a delicious garnish for a baked or roasted filet of beef or for a thick-broiled beefsteak.

Mushrooms

Many persons who like this excellent fungus are afraid to eat it because accidents have occurred from its use, but care will guard against such danger, both with fresh and canned mushrooms. It should be remembered that a perfectly good fungus, which is in excellent eating order when gathered, may decay and become unfit for food in a few hours; therefore all species should be eaten or preserved when fresh.

TEST FOR SAFETY. Form and appearance safely indicate the innocuous or harmful qualities of fresh mushrooms, but the test of tasting may be applied if one need be exercised. If a small part of the cap, eaten with a little salt, does not cause a burning or stinging sensation in the throat or stomach, and if the taste is pleasant and agreeable, the variety may be used. If this test shows the presence of a poisonous matter by the burning sensation, the peril can be averted by a free use of common salt followed by emetics and castor oil. A favorite popular test is to cook with the mushrooms a white onion peeled or a silver spoon and, if either turns black, to avoid the mushrooms as poisonous.

TRY THESE METHODS OF COOKING MUSHROOMS:

❧ *To stew*, cut mushroom stems in rather small pieces and put over the fire with a heaping tablespoonful of butter and a palatable seasoning of salt and pepper to each pint. Stew them gently until they are tender. Have ready delicate toast and serve the mushrooms on it.

❧ *To scallop*, mince the stems and scallop them with an equal quantity of bread crumbs and a palatable seasoning of salt and pepper; brown them in a hot oven.

❧ *To dry*, spread fresh mushrooms after a careful cleaning on sheets of stout paper laid in dripping pans; set the pans in the sun and gradually dry them until all the moisture is evaporated from them. After the mushrooms are dried, thoroughly pack them in a tin can with a tight cover and keep them in a cool, dry place.

Desserts

SELECT DESSERTS BY THE DINNER. When you have a hearty, salt-meat dinner, use a cold, light, delicate pudding, like a boiled custard. When you have a fish dinner, which does not give the nourishment that meat does, serve a boiled, hearty pudding. When you are short of milk, a lemon cornstarch pudding can be used, and a broken cold pudding can be made fresh again by arranging it in a clean dish and covering it with a méringue.

BAKE DEEP CAKES WITH PAPER. When a cake pan is too shallow for the quantity of cake desired, extend it with stiff glazed paper thickly coated with butter; if the oven heat is moderate, the butter will preserve the paper from burning.

DECORATE BIRTHDAY CAKES WITH LETTERS. Reserve about one-quarter of your icing; stir in a drop of cochineal to color it pink. Make a three-cornered paper funnel, put in the icing, and fasten tightly. Take it in your hand as you would a pen, and press with your thumb as you make the letters. The size of the mark depends upon the size of the opening in the paper funnel.

HAVE LIGHTNESS IN MIND WHEN BAKING. Whoever eats heavy pie crust commits a crime against his physical well being, and must pay the penalty. The good housewife should see to it that all pastry and cakes are light; no others should be eaten.

USE A FREEZER TO MAKE ICE CREAM. The secret of making good ice cream of any grade lies in the freezing. The old way of freezing cream, which is still in use among small confectioners, consisted of occasionally stirring the cream while it was freezing in a tin can set in a tub of ice and salt. A more easy and expeditious method is within the reach of the average housekeeper in these days of patent freezers. The principle underlying all the best-known patents is the mixing of the cream by a wooden beater which revolves inside the can by the same motion that slightly changes the position of the can in the outer tub of ice and salt.

COLOR THE CREAM IF YOU WISH. Boil very slowly in a gill of water twenty grains of cochineal and the same of alum and of finely powdered cream of tartar till reduced to half; strain and keep in a phial, tightly corked. For *yellow* coloring, use an infusion of saffron; for *green*, use spinach leaves boiled and the juice expressed; for *red*, express the juice from pokeberries. To every pint, allow a pound of sugar and boil fifteen minutes. A teaspoonful of this jelly will color two quarts of milk.

SET AWAY PLUM PUDDING FOR THE MORROW. If you want to keep plum puddings good for a long time, say some months, hang them in a cold place in the cloth in which they are boiled. When wanted for use, take them out of the cloth, cover them with a clean one, and warm them through with hot water; they will then be fit for the table.

Seasonings and Garnishes

A man is able to work longer and better if his meals are nourishing. He does not know when to add salt or pepper, and why should he? It should be the care of the wife or daughter to so season the food that the first mouthful is appetizing.

Herbs

PREPARE A BOUQUET OF HERBS FOR FLAVOR. Hold a small bunch of parsley in the palm of the left hand; lay on it a small stalk of celery, a bay leaf, a sprig of any sweet herb except sage, a blade of mace, and a dozen peppercorns or a small red-pepper pod; fold the parsley so as to enclose all the other seasonings and tie it in a compact little bundle; this is called a bouquet, or *fagot* of herbs, in French cookbooks, and serves to give an indescribable and delicious flavor to the dishes in which it is cooked.

Relishes

The innumerable small appetizers known as relishes, or hors d'œuvres, include all forms of pickles and table sauces, small sandwiches, and crusts garnished with highly seasoned meats, various preparations of cheese and eggs—in short, any small, highly spiced or seasoned dish calculated to rouse or stimulate the appetite.

CONSIDER THESE RELISHES:

Smoked fish. Small strips of cured fish, either salted or smoked, are acceptable as a relish. Small fish preserved in oil, such as anchovies or sardines, may be wiped dry with a towel and served with vinegar or lemon juice. Smoked eels, herring, halibut, sturgeon, tunny-fish, salt codfish, salmon, Finnan haddie, Yarmouth bloaters, or any dried fish may be served; only it must be delicately prepared in small pieces and with some suitable garnish, so as to be an appreciable incentive to the enjoyment of the heavier dishes which succeed it. Sliced lemon is always a good garnish for any highly seasoned relish.

Sandwich butter. Mix together equal parts of good butter and grated ham or tongue; season it rather highly with salt, cayenne, and mustard mixed with vinegar. Pack the mixture into little earthen jars. Cover each jar with a piece of paper dipped in brandy, and then exclude the air by a tight cover or a bladder wet and then tied over the top, Keep in a cool, dry place. The flavor may be changed by varying the ingredients and seasoning.

❧ *Sandwiches.* Very acceptable sandwiches can be made with the potted and deviled meats and game now sold in jars and tins. The bread should be quite free from crust, cut in thin small slices, and thinly spread with the best butter; a very thin layer of highly seasoned meat, game, poultry, or some kind of spiced or salted fish is put between two slices of buttered bread. Irregular edges are trimmed off and the sandwiches kept cool until served. Meat or fish for sandwiches should be chopped or grated and rather highly seasoned.

❧ *Canapés.* These are small slices of bread slightly hollowed out on the upper surface and then fried golden brown in plenty of hot fat. The little hollow is filled with any highly seasoned meat and the canapés served either hot or cold.

❧ *Puff Pastries.* These are forms of pastry made both in sweets and with delicate force meats and ragouts to be served as hot entrés. Timbales are small patties baked in deep, smooth moulds. Bouchees are very small shells of puff pastry filled with any highly seasoned mince or ragout and served both hot and cold. Rissoles, the smallest puff pastries, are turnovers filled with highly seasoned mince and either baked or fried like croquettes.

Consider Pickles as Relishes and Heed These Pickling Times:

❧ *Oysters* must stand two days covered in stewed juice and vinegar to become pickled.

❧ *Pickle vinegar* ought to be prepared several months before using and always kept on hand ready for use.

❧ Cut and scalded cabbage and chopped and scalded onion for chopped *cabbage pickle* should be covered with boiling brine and left for 24 hours; if it should taste very salty after being squeezed in a cloth, soak in clear water for a few hours and squeeze again.

❧ Three weeks is long enough for *green pickles* to remain in brine, if you wish to make your pickle early in the fall.

❧ *Yellow pickle* must stand for two full days in brine, poured over while hot; on the third day, spread them on a board or table and let them stand in the hot sun four days, taking care that no dew shall fall on them.

❦ *Sweet tomato pickle* will be ready for use in a fortnight after being prepared, poured into a stone jar, and sealed tight.

❦ For *boiled cucumber pickle*, take fresh cucumbers, put them in brine for a few days; take them out, and put them in vinegar to soak for two days.

❦ *Mangoes* must be left in brine two weeks and greened, as you would cucumbers, before being stuffed and covered with vinegar in a jar to be stored.

❦ For *peach mangoes*, repeat the pouring on of syrup for three mornings, boil on the fourth, and wait a few weeks.

❦ *Pepper mangoes* must be packed closely in a stone jar (with the small end downwards) in vinegar for three weeks to be ready for use.

❦ *Walnuts* to be pickled remain in salt water for five or six weeks, then in fresh water for twenty-four hours, and are ready for use in two or three weeks.

❦ Keep *martinas* covered in very strong brine for ten days, then wash and put them in vinegar to stand ten more days before putting them in the jar intended for them.

❦ For *chow-chow*, pack ingredients in salt for a night, soak in vinegar and water for two days, and boil for three mornings.

Pickle and Relish Jars Must be Carefully Sealed

MAKE A SEALING WAX FOR PICKLE JARS. Put three ounces of yellow beeswax into a small tin pail with six ounces of powdered rosin; set the pail in a pan of hot water and stir the wax and rosin until they are melted and smoothly blended. While the wax is still liquid from the action of heat, apply it to the jars or bottles containing pickles or preserves after they are corked.

Spirits

No drinks which contain alcohol in any shape should be used daily, much less semi- or tri-daily by a well person. This principle reduced to practice would prove the preventive that would cure, all over the land, the need for Temperance Societies and Inebriate Asylums.

OCCASIONALLY ENLIVEN ORDINARY DISHES WITH THE ADDITION OF SPIRITS:

- A little brandy will improve *calf's head soup*, though it is a delightful soup as it is.
- Just before serving, add a glass of Madeira wine to *turtle soup*.
- Add brandy and wine to *mock turtle soup*.
- When *rump* or *beef stew* is served up, pour a little wine over it and strew the top with allspice.
- Half an hour before dishing up *beef tongue stew*, add one-half wineglassful wine and seasonings and stew awhile together.
- When the water has nearly stewed away from *rabbit stew*, add half a pint of Port wine and let it stew gently till quite tender.
- Put a little white wine in the stewpan with seasoned half-roasted *pigeons*, a quart of good gravy, and additional seasonings.
- Season *turtle* or *terrapin stew* with champagne or another wine.
- Just before dishing up *calves' feet dressed as terrapins*, add two wineglasses of good cooking wine and simmer again.
- Add a glass of wine just before taking up *tongue a la terrapin*.
- As you remove *turtles* from the fire, pour in one-half pint Madeira wine.

- In preparing *baked calf's head*, add a wineglass of wine to deep dish holding boiled calf's head and seasonings. Fill up the dish with the water the head was boiled in, and bake three-quarters of an hour.

- Just before dinner, put a glass of red wine in *haunch of venison* and let it stew a little longer.

- When *fish salad* is cold, put over it a little Worcestershire sauce and sherry wine.

- Season *tartaric cakes* with mace or wine.

- When ready to boil *English plum pudding*, wet all the ingredients with ten eggs, well-beaten, and two wineglasses of wine and the same of brandy.

- Serve *sippet pudding* hot with a rich sauce made of sugar and butter seasoned with nutmeg and Madeira wine.

- Add one wineglassful wine to recipe for *orange pie*.

- The requisite quantity of pale Madeira or sherry should be added to *jelly, baked custard, creams*, and *Charlotte Russe* after the other ingredients have been well boiled together.

- When preparing *syllabub*, dissolve the sugar in one cupful wine, then pour it on the milk from a height, slowly so as to cause the milk to froth.

- Use one tablespoonful wine of the rennet in making *slip*.

- For *frozen pudding*, put in the wine when syrup is nearly boiling; add last a wineglass of brandy.

- If you like, pour good Madeira or sherry wine over *ambrosia*.

- Mix in to batter for *pancakes* four tablespoonfuls Madeira wine.

- Add brandy to *crab cider*, so much as you think best.

RESTORE WINE THAT HAS TURNED SOUR OR SHARP. Put in a bag the root of wild horseraddish cut in bits. Let it down in the wine, and leave it there two days; take this out, and put another, repeating the same till the wine is perfectly restored. Or fill a bag with wheat for the same effect.

DINNER BILL.

SOUPS.

Mutton Broth 15¢   Macaroni 15¢   Chicken 15¢
Fish or Clam Chowder 15¢

FISH.

Fish Balls, single, 10¢,   Fried Halibut or Cod 30¢
Fresh or Salt Mackerel 30¢   Broiled Halibut or Cod 30¢

BOILED.

Corned Pork and vegetables 30¢   Corned Beef and vegetables 35¢
Cold Tongue 35¢   Cold Ham 30¢   Cold Corned Beef 30¢

ROAST.

Turkey 50¢   Spring Chicken 50¢   Sirloin Beef 45¢
Rib Beef 35¢   Stuffed Veal 35¢   Roast Lamb 30¢

FRIED.

Fried Veal Steak 30¢   Beef Steak and Onions 50¢
Lamb Chop 35¢   Fried Salt Pork and Apples 30¢
Liver 25¢   Tripe in Batter 35¢   Fried Potatoes 10¢

VEGETABLES.

Dressed Celery 10¢   Sweet Potatoes 10¢
Stewed Tomatoes 10¢   New Squash 5¢   Boiled Onions 5¢
Mashed Turnips 5¢   Mashed Potatoes 5¢   Beets 5¢

—menu selctions from Knox Co.'s Horticultural Dining Rooms,
No. 61 Bromfield St., Boston, 1896

PART FOUR

The Hostess and Cook

CHAPTER ONE

Easily Done: Recipes to Use at Family Table for Breakfast, Luncheon, and Supper

BREADS

Bread-making can be cultivated to any extent as a fine art, and the various kinds of biscuit, tea-rusks, twists, and rolls, into which bread may be made, are much better worth a housekeeper's ambition than the getting-up of rich and expensive cake or confections.

—Harriet Beecher Stowe, *House and Home Papers*, 1869

Boston Brown Bread

Steam 3 ½ cups Indian corn meal, 2 ½ cups rye meal (not flour), 2 teaspoonfuls soda, dissolved in 1 quart milk (either sweet or sour) and ⅔ cup molasses in a tin pudding boiler for 5 hours. Take off the cover,

Tea at Breakfast

Of late, the introduction of English breakfast tea has raised a new sect among the tea-drinkers, reversing some of the old canons. Breakfast tea must be boiled! Unlike the delicate article of olden time, which required only a momentary infusion to develop its richness, this requires a longer and severer treatment to bring out its strength—thus confusing all the established usages, and throwing the work into the hands of the cook in the kitchen. The faults of tea, as too commonly found at our hotels and boarding-houses, are that it is made in every way the reverse of what it should be. The water is hot, perhaps, but not boiling; the tea has a general flat, stale, smoky taste, devoid of life or spirit; and it is served, usually, with thin milk, instead of cream. Cream is as essential to the richness of tea as of coffee.

—Harriet Beecher Stowe, *House and Home Papers*, 1869

and set in the oven with the beans to remain till morning.

—*Mrs. Winslow's Domestic Receipt Book*, 1878

Parker House Corn Cake

Mix 1 cup flour, 1 cup corn meal, ½ cup sugar, 1½ teaspoons cream tartar, 1 teaspoonful soda, ½ teaspoonful salt and sift. Melt an egg-sized lump of butter in 1 cup of warm milk and add 1 beaten egg and ½ cup sugar. Pour liquid mixture into dry mixture and beat well. Bake in buttered pans or gem tins in a brisk oven.

—Sarah G. Lambert, Lowell, MA, *Our Cook Book*, 1910

Sally Lunn

Sift together 1 pint flour, 2 tablespoonsful sugar, and a little salt. Warm 1 cup milk and melt in 2 tablespoonsful Cottonlene. Stir into the flour, adding also the ½ cake compressed yeast dissolved in a little lukewarm water. Beat very well; add 1 egg, yolk and white beaten separately. Pour all into buttered cake pan and let rise until double its bulk—about 2 hours. Sprinkle lightly with granulated sugar and bake in a moderately hot oven. Serve warm, cut into squares. If set overnight for breakfast, ¼ as much yeast is required.

—*Home Helps*, 1910

Breakfast Menus

Plums and Pears
Cracked Wheat with Sugar and Cream
Baked Beans   Fish Balls   Brown Bread
Coffee

Peaches
Farinose with Sugar and Cream
Omelet   Potatoes à la Maître d'Hôtel   Berry Muffins
Coffee

—*Boston Cooking-School Cook Book*, 1896

Excellent Light Biscuits

Boil 4 large Irish potatoes. While hot, mash them with egg-sized lump of lard. Add 1 teacup milk and 1 teacup yeast. Stir in enough flour to make a good batter (about 2 quarts) and set it to rise. When light, make up the dough. You generally have to add more water or milk. Roll thick, let them rise slowly, but bake them quickly.

Practical American Cookery, 1885

Breakfast Waffles

Beat well 9 eggs. Dissolve 1 tespoonful soda in milk, then strain. Sift 2 teaspoonsful cream tartar with enough flour to make the batter as thick as pound cake batter.

—*Mrs. Winslow's Domestic Receipt Book*, 1878

English Muffins

Scald a pint of milk, and when lukewarm stir in 3 cups sifted flour and 1 teaspoonful salt; beat hard and add melted butter, 4 ounces, then ½ cake compressed yeast dissolved in a gill of warm water, and beat again. Let stand covered in a warm place until very light. If wanted for tea at 6 o'clock, mix about half-past two. Butter some muffin rings and lay on a hot griddle; half-fill with the batter and bake until brown on one side, then turn and brown on the other; remove the rings and let them remain over a slow fire for a moment or two. Tear (never cut) them open, drop in some butter, lay together and serve at once. If any are left until cold, toast and butter them.

—*Healy & Bigelow's New Cook Book*, 1890

Cream Fritters

Put into a double boiler 1 pint milk and 1 pint Quaker Oats; stir until each grain is moistened with milk. Cover the kettle, and cook slowly for 1 hour. Add ½ cup sugar and 1 teaspoonful of vanilla, and turn into a square pan to cool. When cold, cut into strips the length of your finger and one inch wide. Dip in egg and then in bread crumbs and fry in smoking hot fat. Drain on brown paper, dust with powdered sugar, and serve hot.

—*Cereal Foods and How to Cook Them*, 1899

MILK TOAST. *Milk Toast, to be nice, must be crisp, brown, and tender but not so soft that the cream will soak into it; care should be taken that the milk be in readiness when the toast is made, so that the toast will not have time to steam before the milk is poured over it. The cream dressing should not be quite so thick as condensed milk but a little thicker than common cream. Corn starch or flour may be used as thickening devices.*

WELSH RAREBIT. *The only difference between Milk Toast and Welsh Rarebit is in the dressing, which for the latter contains a little grated cheese and an egg. Gentlemen usually enjoy Welsh Rare-bit, which can be a very inviting dish for supper.*

STALE BREAD BATTER CAKES. *Put a loaf of stale bread to stand all day in a pint of milk. Just before tea add 3 eggs and 1 large spoon of butter. If too thin, add a little flour.*

BREADING. Stale bread may be laid aside until thoroughly dried, then rolled very fine. Put this into a wide-mouthed bottle into which you can dip a spoon. This is useful in many ways, as in breading veal chops or oysters.

WATER TOAST. *The bread should be nicely browned, then dipped quickly in salted water. Do not spread butter over it, but place little bits to melt; this prevents the toast being broken.*

QUEEN TOAST. *Queen toast is made by soaking the slices in a very plain uncooked custard and browning in a frying pan. When served, sugar and cinnamon are sprinkled between the slices as they are piled upon the dish.*

TOAST CRUMBS. *Toast crumbs are made of buttered bread cut in very small cubes and placed in the oven to brown. These are very nice served with soup, and it is a good way to use up very small pieces of bread.*

—*Cooking Garden*, 1885

Popovers

Beat 2 large or 3 small eggs well; mix carefully 2 cups flour, ½ teaspoonful salt, and 2 cups milk. Pour into hot greased irons and bake in rather hot oven ½ hour or more, according to size. Serve promptly.

—Home Helps, 1910

Grandpa's Favorite Griddle Cakes

Beat 3 eggs well. Mix 1 quart milk and 2 cups stale bread crumbs. Work until smooth; stir in 1 tablespoonful melted butter and eggs; then the salt, 1 teaspoonful; lastly just enough flour to bind the mixture. If too thick, add milk. Take care they do not stick to the griddle.

—Common Sense in the Household, 1871

MEAT STUFFS

Supreme of Halibut

Remove skin and bone from about 1 pound of halibut, then finely chop. There should be 1 cup, or ½ pound, of fish. Add 1 teaspoonful of salt and a dash of white pepper or paprika; then, one at a time, beat in 4 eggs, beating the mixture smooth between each addition. Then beat in 1 pint of cream gradually. Turn the mixture into buttered timbale molds, individual size, or one large mold holding 3 pints. Set on a fold of paper in a dish of hot water, and cook in the oven until the center is firm. It will take 15 or 20 minutes to cook in the small molds, and 1 hour or more in the large mold. Serve with any fish sauce.

Gem-Chopper Cook Book, 1902

At 2 p.m. lunch I commonly invite to that—cup of tea and biscuit and butter with cold meat—any gentleman I wish to have more conference with than is practicable in hours given to miscellaneous business.

—President Rutherford B. Hayes,
from his White House diary, March 18, 1878

Deviled Lobster

Make a cream sauce with 2 tablespoons each of butter and flour and 2 cups milk. Mix the sauce with 2 cups of cut-up lobsters, the juice of one lemon, 2 chopped hard-boiled eggs, and salt and pepper. Fill shells, smooth tops, and sprinkled with sifted crumbs of 3 Boston crackers, rolled. Brown in a quick oven 10 minutes.

—Miss Mary Shattuck, Lowell, MA, *Our Cook Book*, 1910

Boston Fry

Prepare the oysters in egg batter and fine cracker meal; fry in butter over a slow fire for about 10 minutes. Cover the hollow of a hot platter with tomato sauce; place the oysters in it but not covered by it. Garnish with chopped parsley sprinkled over the oysters.

—Boston Oyster House, *White House Cook Book*, 1887

Small Oyster Pies

For each pie, take a tin plate half the size of an ordinary dinner plate; butter it, and cover the bottom with a puff paste, as for pies. Lay on it select oysters, or enough to cover the bottom; butter them and season with a little salt and plenty of pepper. Spread over this an egg batter, and cover with a crust of the paste, making small openings in it with a fork. Bake in a hot oven 15 to 20 minutes, or until the top is nicely browned.

—Boston Oyster House, *White House Cook Book*, 1887

Fish Balls

Pare 6 medium potatoes and boil ½ hour. Drain off all the water, turn the potatoes into the tray with 1 pint finely chopped, cooked salt fish and mash light and fine with a vegetable masher. Add 1 heaping tablespoonful butter, 1 egg, and 2 tablespoonsful cream or 4 tablespoonsful milk, and pepper then mix thoroughly.

—Earl S. Sloan, Boston, Sloan's Cook Book and Advice to Housekeepers, 1905

Luncheon Menus

Turkey Soup
Veal Loaf and Lettuce Salad
Bavarian Cream

—The Enterprising Housekeeper, 1889

Lobster Salad   Rolls
Raspberries and Cream with Wafers
Russian Tea

—Boston Cooking-School Cook Book, 1896

Veal Loaf

Chop 3 pounds raw veal fine and mix with 1 heaping teaspoonful each of salt and pepper, 2 raw eggs, and about 2 tablespoonsful of water. Mold this into a loaf, then roll it in cracker crumbs, and pour melted butter over it. Place it in a pan and bake 2 hours. To be sliced off when cold.

—*Mrs. Winslow's Domestic Receipt Book,* 1878

Hodge Podge

Put a coffee cup of salt on 4 quarts of chopped green tomatoes and let stand overnight; drain them and add 1 quart chopped onions, 1 coffee cup chopped green peppers, and 1 coffee cup white mustard seed. Cover the whole with cold, sharp vinegar.

—C.I. Hood Apothecaries, Lowell, MA, *Hood's Cook Book Reprint Number One,* 1877

Odds and Ends

Relishes are nowhere more acceptable than upon the luncheon table, but that which deserves the highest consideration for this meal is the utilization of culinary odds and ends. Croquettes, soufflés, meats for sandwiches, and all meat entrees become simplified by means of a meat chopper, and the majority of dishes coming under the head of entrées are but different forms of hash or preparing minced meat.

—Helen Johnson, *The Enterprising Housekeeper,* 1889

Fricandelles

Take meat—the more variety the better—hash it fine, and mix with 2 eggs, grated onion, melted butter, pounded crackers, pepper, and salt. Form into balls, and fry in butter. Serve with drawn butter flavored with lemon.

—C.I. Hood Apothecaries, Lowell, MA, *Hood's Cook Book Reprint Number One,* 1877

VEGETABLES, TOO

Boston Baked Beans

Soak 1 quart of beans overnight, pour off the water, and cook in fresh water until they crack open. Then put into a deep earthen dish and cover with the water. Add molasses, about ⅓ of a cup, and put into center of the dish a pound of parboiled pork, which should be scored across the rind. Bake very slowly 4 hours. Keep nearly covered with water until two thirds done; then let them bake brown.

—Mrs. Charles P. Searle, Boston, *Famous Old Receipts*, 1906

Currant Catsup for Baked Beans

To the juice from 5 pints of strained currants, add 3 pounds sugar (brown will do nicely), 1 pint vinegar, 1 tablespoonful cinnamon, 1 tablespoonful pepper, 1 tablespoonful cloves, 1 tablespoonful allspice, ½ tablespoonful salt. Scald the mixture well ¾ hour, then put in bottles and cork tight; it will keep for years. As farmers generally have a quantity of currants that go to waste, I would like them to try this, and I think they will never be sorry.

—Massachusetts Ploughman, *Dr. Chase's Third Last and Complete Receipt Book and Household Physician*, 1903

Broiled Tomatoes

Wipe, scald, peel, cut in halves, and lay on a wire broiler. When hot add a bit of butter, pepper, and salt and serve when brown. Or, sprinkle the tomatoes with buttered crumbs before broiling.

—*Home Helps*, 1910

Macaroni Casserole

Boil a pound of macaroni for an hour. Drain and mix with ½ pound macaroni, ½ pound slice American or Canadian cheese, ¼ pound diced bacon, ½ can tomatoes or 4 freshly sliced tomatoes, 1½ teaspoonful salt, and ⅛ teaspoonful pepper. Put in a casserole dish oiled with bacon fat, and add a little milk or water if the mixture seems dry. Cover and bake in a slow oven.

—*"New Process" Wick Oil Cook Stove Cook Book*, ca. 1910s

Sweet Potato Dish

Arrange layers of 4 to 5 sliced sweet potatoes and slices of unpeeled orange in a buttered 1½ quart glass casserole dish. Dot with butter; sprinkle with brown sugar. Place slices of unpeeled orange over the top. Add water, and bake with cover on.

—Edith Nourse Rogers, First U.S. Congresswoman from Massachusetts,
Favorite Recipes of Famous 'Daughters'

Saratoga Potatoes

Peel and slice thin the potatoes and place into cold water. Drain well, and dry in a towel. Fry a few at a time in hot Cottolene. Salt as you take them out, and lay them on coarse brown paper for a short time. They are very nice cold for lunch or to take to picnics.

—*Home Helps*, 1910

Winter Succotash

This may be made with limas, horticulturals, garden beans, or white field beans. The latter are seldom used for succotash, but they make it very nicely. The method of proceeding in each case is the same. Boil the beans without soaking until three-fourths done. In the meantime put an equal amount of dried sweet corn with 3 quarts water, and let it steep on the stove for 2 hours without boiling, then add to it the beans, and let them cook together gently until the beans are done. Serve warm and do not break the beans.

—A.W. Chase, *Dr. Chase's Third Last and Complete Receipt Book and Household Physician*, 1903

Corn and Cheese Soufflé

Melt 1 tablespoon butter and cook 1 tablespoon pepper thoroughly in it. Make a sauce out of a cup of flour, 2 cups milk, and 1 cup grated cheese; add 1 cup chopped corn, 3 egg yolks, and seasoning. Cut and fold in the egg whites beaten stiffly; turn into a buttered baking dish and bake over a medium flame 30 minutes.

—*"New Process" Wick Oil Cook Stove Cook Book*, ca. 1910s

Potatoes á la Maître d'Hotel

Boil 1 pint of potato balls, cut with a vegetable cutter. Boil in salted water about 10 minutes, drain and pour over them with 1 pint of hot milk, and when the milk is partly absorbed, stir in quickly 1 egg yolk, beaten to a cream, with 2 tablespoonsful butter, 1 tablespoonful lemon juice, 1 tablespoonful minced parsley, ½ teaspoonful salt, and 1 pinch paprika. Serve as soon as the sauce thickens.

—*Home Helps*, 1910

Mock Oysters

Add 2 tablespoonsful cream, ½ teaspoonful salt, ½ teaspoonful pepper, 1 teaspoonful Worcestershire sauce or catsup to 1 cupful of cooked, mashed parsnips, then an egg and 4 rolled soda crackers. Let stand 30 minutes, then form into oyster-shaped patties and dip the patties in slightly beaten egg, diluted with ¼ cup water to each egg, and then dip in dry bread crumbs. Fry in deep fat like oysters. Serve with catsup and cold slaw. Leftover creamed parsnips may be used by omitting the cream on this list of ingredients.

—*"New Process" Wick Oil Cook Stove Cook Book*, ca. 1910s

Rice Croquettes

Boil 1 teacup rice in a pint of milk and a pint of water. When boiled and hot, add an egg-sized drop of butter, 2 tablespoonsful sugar, 2 eggs, and the juice and grated peel of a lemon. Stir this up well; have ready the yolks of 2 more eggs beaten on a plate, and cracker crumbs on another. Make the rice in rolls and dip the rolls in the egg and crumbs; fry them in butter; serve hot.

—*Mrs. Winslow's Domestic Receipt Book*, 1878

Supper Menus

Shrimp Salad   Saratoga Potatoes
Brown Bread and Butter Sandwiches   Coffee
Lemon Jelly Wafers

Steamed Clams with Butter Sauce
Veal Loaf   Spiced Currants
Cake   Iced Tea   Orange Sherbet

Broiled Tomatoes   Potato Croquettes
Peach Shortcake
Chocolate

—*The Enterprising Housekeeper*, 1889

EGGS & CHEESE

Eggs à la Virginia

Take the yolks and whites of six eggs, beaten separately. Melt a lump of butter in the chafing dish. Mix the whites and yolks, beating together and seasoning to taste. Have ready some small pieces of sweetbread, and stir all together in the chafing dish until cooked. Serve on toast.

—Charles Dana Gibson, creator of the Gibson-Girls,
Roxbury, MA, *Favorite Food of Famous Folk,* 1900

Shirred Eggs in Shredded Wheat Biscuit Baskets

Turn a cup of milk into a shallow dish. Prepare the biscuit baskets by crushing an oblong cavity in the top of 6 shredded-wheat biscuits with a teaspoon and removing the inside shreds. Dip the bottom of the basket lightly in the milk and place in buttered pan. Put little bits of butter in the bottom of biscuit baskets, salt and pepper lightly, and break an egg into each basket. Put little bits of butter on top, salt and pepper, set in moderate oven until white of the egg is set. Remove from pan with pancake turner to warm plate and serve at once.

—*The Vital Question Cook Book,* 1908

Deviled Ham with Egg Vermicelli

Make a white sauce with 2 tablespoonsful each of butter and flour, ¼ teaspoonful salt, and 1 cup rich milk. Mix this gradually with ¼–½ cup Underwood Deviled Ham; when smooth, add the whites of 4 hard-boiled eggs, chopped rather coarse. Let heat over hot water, then spread upon 4 to 5 slices of bread, toasted after the removal of the crust, with the edges slightly moistened in boiling salted water. Pass the yolks of the eggs through a sieve upon the top of the ham-and-egg mixture. Garnish with parsley and serve.

—Janet M. Hill, Boston, *Taste the Taste and Some Cookery News*, ca. 1910s

Eggs in Disguise

Make a paste with 1 cup fine bread crumbs, a beaten egg, 2 table-spoonsful Underwood Deviled Ham, and ½ cup of milk, or enough to moisten. Line buttered cups with this, and drop an egg from its shell into the center. Bake or steam until the eggs are firm—all the better if the yolk is hard. Loosen from the cup and turn each out on a small square of buttered toast. This quantity is sufficient for 4 to 6 eggs.

—Boston Cooking-School, *Taste the Taste and Some Cookery News*, ca. 1910s

Flour Drop Cakes

Beat 4 eggs to a froth, melt ½ cup butter and turn upon the eggs with a pint of new milk and 2 tablespoonsful sugar; then stir in 4 ½ cups flour flour, and bake in earthen cups 1 hour.

Ransom's Family Receipt Book, 1885

Cheese Patties

Make white sauce of butter and flour, add milk and beaten yolk of 2 eggs; season, grate in American cheese, and set away to cool. Make pastry cases, and when ready to serve, beat your egg whites light and fold into cheese mixture. Put into cases, heat, and serve immediately.

—Mrs. Henry Parkman, Boston, *Famous Old Receipts,* 1906

Picadie for the Chafing Dish

Mix 2 tablespoons butter, a little onion, 1 can of chicken (chopped), 1 can of mushrooms, ½ can of tomatoes without the liquid, and ½ cup

Summer Feast

*A*nd the offerings [of summer] arrive with such glorious progressiveness! First comes the strawberry, like a blush on the cheek of Mother Earth; then the berries and vegetables of more vigorous growth; then the stately, luscious melon, the charm and glory of the breakfast table; then corn, which is meat in nutrition; then the juicy apple, the pride of prince and peasant. Then we come to the pear and to the orchard—

Where peaches grow with sunny dyes,
Like maiden's cheeks when blushes rise,
Where huge figs the branches bend.
Where clusters from the vine distend.

There is the feast which nature spreads. Let every man say grace in his heart and partake of it thankfully.

—A.W. Chase, *Dr. Chase's Third Last and Complete Receipt Book and Household Physician,* 1903

cream. Heat in chafing dish. Add seasoning and then 3 lightly beaten eggs.

—Mrs. Mary S. Cushing, *Our Cook Book,* Lowell, MA, 1910

Irish Monkeys

Soak 1 cup bread crumbs in milk for half an hour. Melt a walnut-sized piece of butter in a chafing dish or double broiler; add soaked crumbs, 1 cup melted cheese, cayenne, and 1 well-beaten egg. Serve on hot toast.

—Catherine M. Smith, *Our Cook Book,* Lowell, MA, 1910

Welsh Rarebit

Heat 1 cup milk. Beat 1 egg and add it to 1 teaspoonful flour, ½ teaspoonful salt, ½ teaspoonful mustard, and 6 tablespoons grated cheese. Stir all into hot milk. When thick, add butter and serve on saltines.

—Mrs. Freda Fox, *Our Cook Book,* Lowell, MA, 1910

SALADS & FRUITS

Orange Salad

Cut up Sunkist oranges, removing seeds and white fiber. Mix with a little sugar and serve with a cream dressing made by mixing ½ cup vinegar, ½ teaspoonful salt, ½ cup sugar, 1 dash cayenne, and 3 egg yolks. Put in double boiler, stirring constantly until creamy. Beat in frothy whites while mixture is still hot, then remove from fire. Put away to cool and add 2 cups sweet or sour cream.

—Recipes for Dainty Dishes, ca. 1910s

Cream Slaw

Put 1 pint vinegar, ½ cup sugar, and a walnut-sized piece of butter in a saucepan and let boil; stir 2 eggs, a pint of sour cream, and 1 teaspoonful of flour, previously well mixed, into the vinegar. Boil thoroughly and throw over 1 gallon of finely cut cabbage, previously sprinkled with 1 teaspoonful each of salt, black pepper, and mustard.

—Centennial Buckeye Cookbook, 1876

Tomato Jelly

Soak ½ ounce of gelatin in ½ cup water. Boil 2 cups tomatoes, 1 slice of onion, 1 bay leaf, ½ teaspoonful thyme, ¼ teaspoonful pepper, 1 teaspoonful salt, 1 teaspoonful sugar, and 3 cloves until tomatoes are soft. Mix with a salad dressing, mould, and serve with celery.

—Caroline A. Durant, Lowell, MA, *Our Cook Book,* 1910

Salad á la Red Devil

Chop together lettuce, celery and tomato. Make a dressing by boiling together 1 egg, 1 tablespoonful butter, ½ cup vinegar, salt, pepper, and mustard. When thickened, stir in 2 tablespoonsful Underwood Deviled Ham. Pour mixture over the salad and serve on lettuce leaves.

—Taste the Taste and Some Cookery News, ca. 1910s

Italian Salad

Cook and slice one turnip and one carrot; when cold, mix them with 2 sliced boiled potatoes and 1 slice beet root. Add a very little onion and cover mixture with dressing.

—International Health Resort Recipes, ca. 1900s

Lobster Salad

Cook in a bowl set in a kettle of water 1 tablespoonful sugar, 2 tablespoonsful butter, 1 tablespoonful salt, 2 tablespoonsful vinegar, and 1 tablespoonful mustard, stirring until it thickens. When cold, add cream enough to make as thin as boiled custard. Beat the whites of 4 eggs separately and add last. Add salt and red pepper. Serve over chopped lobster and lettuce.

—C.I. Hood Apothecaries, Lowell, MA, *Hood's Cook Book Reprint Number One,* 1877

Chow-Chow

A peck of tomatoes, 2 quarts of green peppers, ½ peck of onions, 2 cabbages cut as for slaw, and 2 quarts of mustard seed. Have a large firkin, put in a layer of sliced tomatoes, then one of onions, next one of peppers, lastly cabbage; sprinkle over some of the mustard seed, repeat the layers again, and so on until you have used up the above quantity. Boil 1 gallon of vinegar, with a bit of alum, 2 ounces of cloves and 2 ounces of allspice tied in a little bag; skim it well and turn into the firkin. Let it stand 24 hours, then pour the whole into a large kettle, and let it boil 5 minutes; turn into the firkin, and stand away for future use.

—*Sweet Home Cook Book,* 1888

Herring Salad

Soak 3 Holland herrings overnight, cut in very small pieces, cook and peel 8 medium potatoes, and chop with 2 small, cooked red beets, 2 onions, a few sour apples, some roasted veal, and 3 hard-boiled eggs. Mix with a sauce of sweet oil, vinegar, broth, pepper, and mustard to taste. A spoonful of thick sour cream improves the sauce, which should stand overnight in an earthen dish.

—*Centennial Buckeye Cookbook,* 5876

Summer Supper

Except in the heat of summer, a hot dish should always be served for supper... Soups are rarely served. Shellfish served raw, or cooked in any form; small fish, broiled or fried; and broiled steaks, chops or chicken, all these are acceptable, especially when a hearty supper is required. But here, as with luncheon, made-over dishes are most often used. Potatoes, rice, hominy, and tomatoes in special forms, such as croquettes, scallops, etc., are served; other vegetables rarely, if ever.

Eggs, salads, and sandwiches in any form, hot breads, griddle cakes, and waffles, all these belong to supper.

—Helen Johnson, *The Enterprising Housekeeper,* 1889

Let's Have a Little Joy Ride

...in the Underwood fairy-land, where everything is in "good taste" and everybody says "Taste the taste."

Here goes for the ride. Hold on tight or you may get spilled at the curves.

To the Waldorf went one of the newly rich; in search of good taste was he. Unable to understand the "manoo," he said unto the waiter, "Bring me $25 worth of ham and eggs." Ham was the best taste he knew—wise raw recruit of the newly rich.

And when you really think it over, is there any taste that actually does taste as good as ham? There is not.

And, in sooth, what could make a taster taste tastier than good boiled ham and 42 spices all ground up fine? That's what Underwood Deviled Ham is, and that's one reason why it tastes good.

However, all ham hasn't the said described taste. Some hams taste good and some taste punk.

But Underwood Ham has the taste—the home ham taste that you got from the farm-cured hams of your girlhood "on the old Brandy-wine."

—Taste the Taste and Some Cookery News,
from W.M. Underwood Co., 52 Fulton Street, Boston
"First Canners in America"

Chapter Two

Recipes Fit to Serve at Dinners: Soups and Meats

DINNER SOUPS

Egg Balls for Soups

Boil 4 eggs 10 minutes. Drop into cold water, and when cool, remove the yolks. Pound these in a mortar until reduced to a paste, and then beat them with 1 teaspoonful of salt, a speck of pepper, and the white of one raw egg. Form into balls about the size of a walnut. Roll in flour and fry brown in butter or chicken fat, being careful not to burn them.

—Earl S. Sloan, Boston, *Sloan's Cook Book and Advice to Housekeepers*, 1905

Clam Soup

Take 50 clams, and if not already opened, put them in a large pan or tray and pour boiling water on them. This will open the shells. Take them out as fast as they unclose, that you may save all the liquor they contain. Cut off the necks and boil for 1 hour in a little water. Strain and lay aside the clams. Put the liquor over the fire again with 12 whole peppers, a few bits of cayenne, 6 blades of mace, and salt to taste. Let it boil for 10 minutes, strain out the spices, then put in the clams and boil 30 minutes, keeping closely covered. Next add milk, which has been heated in the double boiler. Boil up again, taking care the soup does not burn, and put in a tablespoon of flour stirred into a paste with a little cold milk and a tablespoon of butter.

—Edward Everett Hale, Writer and Clergyman, *Favorite Food of Famous Folk,* 1900

Oyster Bisque

Sauté a chopped onion, ½ cup chopped celery and leeks, a bay leaf, and a few pepper berries in butter. When browned, add 2 cups of flour, the juice from 1 quart of oysters, and 1 quart of chicken broth (or any meat stock). Simmer 1 hour. Strain through fine sieve and add cream. Reheat, add 1 tablespoonful of butter and season with salt and cayenne. Cut oysters in small pieces and serve with the soup. (Cheese straws are nice served with this bisque.)

—Ambassador Hotel, Chicago, *Cuisine,* 1912

Fish Chowder

Skin 5 pounds of any kind fish, and cut all the flesh from the bones. Then simmer the bones gently for 10 minutes. Fry ½ pound of pork; add 2 large, sliced onions. Cover and cook 5 minutes; then add 2 tablespoons flour and cook 8 minutes longer, stirring often. Strain on this the water in which the fish bones were cooked, and boil gently for 5 minutes; then strain all on the potatoes and fish. Season with pepper and salt and simmer 15 minutes. Add a pint of milk and crackers, which you should first soak for 3 minutes in the milk. Let it boil up once and serve. A pint of tomatoes can take the place of the milk, if you like.

—Earl S. Sloan, Boston, *Sloan's Cook Book and Advice to Housekeepers*, 1905

Irish Potato Soup

Peel and boil 8 medium potatoes with sliced onion, herbs, salt, and pepper; press all through a colander. Then thin the soup with rich milk and add butter (and more seasoning, if necessary). Let it heat well and serve hot.

—*White House Cook Book*, 1887

Consommé Vivieurs

Cut a heaping cup each of beets, leeks, and celery in Julienne (strips). Parboil in salted water, and finish cooking in consommé. Add the breast of a boiled chicken, also cut in Julienne. Chop a raw beet, press out the juice, and add to the consommé to give it a reddish color.

—*Cuisine*, 1912

Pea Soup

Take ¼ pint peas, 1 small strip salt pork, 1 saltspoon salt, Celery seed, and 1 small piece onion. Fry the piece of onion till brown. Mix all ingredients, cover closely, and boil together 4 or 5 hours. Run through a colander before serving.

—*Cooking Garden*, 1885

Dinner Menus

Macaroni Soup
Fricassee of Lamb   Riced Potatoes   Stewed Tomatoes
String Bean and Radish Salad
Fruit and Nuts

Cream of Celery Soup
Roast Beef   Franconia Potatoes   Yorkshire Pudding
Macaroni with Cheese   Tomato and Lettuce Salad
Chocolate Cream   Café Noir

—Fannie Merritt Farmer's *Boston-Cooking-School Cook Book*, 1896

Spring Soup
Broiled Beefsteak   Royal Croquettes
Mashed Potatoes   Parsnips with Cream Sauce
Lettuce, Mayonnaise Dressing
Minnie's Lemon Pie   Nuts and Raisins

Green Corn Soup
Mutton Cutlets, Tomato Sauce   Potato Duchesse
Cucumber Salad   Scalloped Tomatoes
Curds and Cream

—Ransom's *Family Receipt Book*, 1885

DINNER MEATS

Lobster a la Newburg

Take the nicest part of one large lobster, cut in small slices, and put in chafing dish with a tablespoonful of butter, season well with pepper and salt, pour 1 gill of wine over it. Cook 10 minutes. Add the beaten yolks of 3 eggs and ½ pint of cream. Let it come to a boil and serve immediately.

—Earl S. Sloan, Boston, *Sloan's Cook Book and Advice to Housekeepers*, 1905

Fricassee of Veal

Dredge 1 ½ pound veal steak cut from round with seasoned flour and fry in hot fat on bottom of pressure cooker until light brown. Add 1 onion, 2 stalks celery, and a sliced carrot. Cook for 15 minutes at 15 pound pressure. Take meat up on platter and place vegetables around it. Add 1 cup boiling water and 2 tablespoonsful fat to the juice in which the meat has been cooked. Thicken with 2 tablespoonsful flour.

—*"Kook Kwick" Pressure Cooker Recipes*, ca. 1910s

Stewed Chicken

Divide a chicken into pieces by the joints, and put into a stew pan, with salt, pepper, some parsley, and thyme. Pour in 1 quart of water, with a piece of butter, and when it has stewed an hour and a half, take the chicken out of the pan. If there is no gravy, put in another piece of butter, add some water and flour, and let it boil a few minutes. When done, it should not be quite as thick as drawn butter. For the dumplings: take 1 quart of sifted flour, one teaspoonful of salt, two of cream of tartar and one of soda; mix with milk and form into biscuit; place them upon a tin in a steamer over the kettle where the chicken is boiling. They will steam in 20 minutes. You can rub a little butter in the flour, if you wish them very nice.

—*Sweet Home Cook Book*, 1888

Fillet of Haddock

Melt 1 tablespoonful butter; add 1 tablespoonful flour and salt, pepper, and mustard to taste; and mix to a smooth paste. Add 1 cup milk and cook, stirring constantly, until thickened. Add 1 cup of grated cheese and pour mixture over raw haddock fillets, which have been put in bread pan or casserole, and bake until brown.

—Mrs. H. H. A. Beach, composer and soloist with Boston Symphony Orchestra
Famous Recipes of Famous 'Daughters'

Broiled Halibut

Season halibut slices with salt and pepper, and lay them in melted butter for 30 minutes, covering them well on both sides. Roll in flour and broil for 12 minutes over a clear fire. Serve on a hot dish, garnished with parsley and slices of lemon. The slices of halibut should be about 1 inch thick, and for every pound there should be 3 tablespoonsful of butter.

—Earl S. Sloan, Boston, *Sloan's Cook Book and Advice to Housekeepers*, 1905

Royal Croquettes

Let 3 small or 2 large sweetbreads stand in boiling water 5 minutes. Chop very fine, with one boiled chicken, and add one teaspoonful mace and salt and pepper. Put 2 tablespoonsful butter in a stewpan with a heaping tablespoonful flour. When it bubbles, gradually add a pint of cream. Then add the chopped mixture, and stir until thoroughly heated. Take from the fire, add the juice from half a lemon, and set away to cool. Salt and pepper the cracker crumbs and bread crumbs; roll croquettes into shape with the cracker crumbs. Dip in 6 beaten eggs and then in cracker crumbs. Let stand until dry, then dip again in egg, and finally in bread crumbs—not too fine. Fry quickly in boiling fat.

—Ransom's Family Receipt Book, 1885

Beefsteak Pie

Put 2 pound uncooked meat cut in 1 inch cubes in deep puddingdish and sprinkle over them a tablespoonful of parsley and one onion, both chopped fine, a teaspoonful of salt, and ¼ teaspoonful pepper. To ¼ pound suet freed of membrane and chopped fine, add 1 cup flour, a pinch of salt, and sufficient ice water to moisten but not to make wet. Knead a little until it can be rolled out in a crust large enough to cover the top of the pudding dish. Pour 1 cup Swift's beef extract or stock boiling hot over the meat. Spread the crust over the meat and cut a slit in the top. Brush over with milk and bake in a moderate oven.

—The Kitchen Encyclopedia, 1911

Corned Beef

Wash a piece of corned beef and, if very salty, put it into cold water. Such a piece as one finds in town or city shops, and which the butchers corn themselves, put directly into boiling water. Cook very slowly for 6 hours. This time is for a piece weighing 8 or 10 pound. When it is to be served cold, let it stand for 1 or 2 hours in the water in which it was boiled. If the beef is to be pressed, get either a piece of brisket, flank, or rattle-ran. Take out the bones, place in a flat dish or platter, put a tin sheet on top, and lay on it 2 or 3 bricks. If you have a corned beef press, use that of course.

—Earl S. Sloan, Boston, Sloan's Cook Book and Advice to Housekeepers, 1905

Leg of Mutton Stuffed

Wash and wipe the mutton. Grate a pint of bread crumbs, season with salt and pepper, a teaspoonful of sweet marjoram, two of sage and a half one of sweet basil (all dried and rubbed fine). Chop a medium-sized onion, and put it over the fire in a small saucepan with butter the size of a large egg. Stew for five minutes, pour over the bread crumbs, and stir them in thoroughly. Make a deep incision on the long side of he leg parallel with the bone and push the dressing in, all through the length of the leg. Skewer it at the opening where it was stuffed and season the leg with pepper and salt. Dust it with flour and roast it two hours in a hot oven, keeping a little water in the pan to baste it with every 15 or 20 minutes. Thicken the gravy with browned flour. To be eaten with a currant jelly.

—*Sweet Home Cook Book,* 1888

Spring Chicken Tirolienne

Joint the chicken, dust lightly with flour, and brown in plenty of butter, turning frequently so it will become brown on all sides. Add to it some boiled ham and diced fresh tomatoes, shallot, or onion chopped very fine. Simmer until tender. Garnish with fried apples and chopped parsley. Serve very hot.

—Ambassador Hotel, Chicago *Cuisine,* 1912

CHAPTER THREE

$\mathcal{R}$ECIPES FOR DESSERTS AND BEVERAGES

DINNERTIME DESSERTS

Pineapple Bavarian Cream

Soak ½ package of gelatin 2 hours in ½ cup cold water. Chop a pint of pineapple fine and put it on with a small teacup of sugar. Simmer 20 minutes. Add the gelatin, and strain immediately into a tin basin. Rub as much of the pineapple as possible through the sieve. Beat until it begins to thicken, and add a pint of cream, whipped to a froth. When well mixed, pour into the mold, and put away to harden. Serve with whipped cream.

—Earl S. Sloan, Boston, *Sloan's Cook Book and Advice to Housekeepers*, 1905

Menu

Cotuit Oysters   Cream of Tomatoes
Radishes   Consommé Imperial   Olives
Fried Smelts, Tartar Sauce
Fillet of Beef, Sauce Béarnaise
Roast Stuffed Chicken
Roast Goose
Pear Fritters Glacé, Benedictine
Roast Teal Duck on Toast
Lettuce Salad
Thin Fried Potatoes
Frozen Pudding   Peach Méringue
Charlotte Russe   Ice Cream
Sherbet   Fruit   Cheese
Coffee

—Menu for Meeting of the Massachusetts Reform Club meeting at
Young's Hotel, Boston, September 28, 1899

Strawberry Ice

Mix 1½ cups sugar and 4 cups water, add 2 cups berries mashed and
squeezed through double cheesecloth, and a tablespoon lemon juice;
strain and freeze.

—*Catering for Special Occasions*, 1911

Peanut Drops

Cream 2 tablespoon butter, add ¼ cup sugar and an egg well beaten. Mix and sift a teaspoonful baking powder, ¼ teaspoonful salt, and ½ cup flour; add to first mixture; then add 2 tablespoon milk and ½ cup finely chopped peanuts. Drop from a teaspoon on a slightly buttered sheet 1 inch apart, and place 1 peanut half on top of each. Bake 12 to 15 minutes in a slow oven.

—Catering for Special Occasions, 1911

Peach Tapioca Pudding

Soak ½ pint of tapioca in cold water for 2 or 3 hours, then set on the stove until it boils. Sweeten with white sugar. Peel and slice ripe peaches to nearly fill a baking dish. Sprinkle over them white sugar, then pour over the tapioca, and bake slowly for one hour. To be eaten with cream and sugar.

—Sweet Home Cook Book, 1888

Charlotte Russe No. 3

Soak ¼ box gelatine in cold water. Whip a pint of cream stiff and add 1 cup sugar and 1 teaspoonful vanilla. Dissolve gelatine in milk and strain into whipped cream. Stir occassionally until it begins to stiffin, then pour in a mould lined with sponge cake or lady fingers.

—Mrs. G.H. Scribner, Our Cook Book, 1910

Apple Fritters

Beat 3 eggs lightly and stir in 1 teaspoonful salt, 1 of sugar, and the grated rind of half of a lemon and its juice. Also add 1 pint of milk, 2 cups of chopped apple, and 2 cups of flour. Stir it all well together, and fry, or you can bake it on a griddle as pancakes. Sift sugar over them and send to the table.

—Sweet Home Cook Book, 1888

Delicious Desserts for Summer and Autumn Dinners

Summer

SUNDAY
Fruit Cream
Angel's Food
Roman Punch
Almond Drops

MONDAY
Cherry Pie

TUESDAY
Peach Cottage Pudding
Hard Sauce

WEDNESDAY
Strawberry Shortcake

THURSDAY
Strawberry Sherbet
White Pound Cake

FRIDAY
Charlotte Russe
Ring Jumbles

SATURDAY
Peach Pie

Autumn

SUNDAY
Peach Ice Cream
Caramel Cake

MONDAY
Railroad Pudding
Foaming Sauce

TUESDAY
Custard Pie

WEDNESDAY
Velvet Blanc Mange
Sugar Cookies

THURSDAY
Pumpkin Pie

FRIDAY
Coconut Pie

SATURDAY
Apple Fritters
White Wine Sauce

—Price's Delicious Desserts, 1904

ASSORTED OTHER
CONFECTIONS

Hermits

Mix 2 cups brown sugar, 2 eggs well beaten, ¾ cup butter and lard mixed, 1 tablespoonful cinnamon, 1 teaspoonful each soda dissolved in milk and cloves, 6 tablespoonsful sour milk, and 1 cup each chopped raisins and walnuts. Add flour to make it stiff enough to drop from a spoon. Bake in buttered tins.

—*Cupid at Home in the Kitchen,* ca. 1910

Ginger Snaps

Boil a cup of molasses and stir in 1 tablespoonful butter, 1 tablespoonful ginger, and 1 teaspoonful saleratus, rolled fine. Stir flour in while hot. Roll out thin, cut, and bake.

—A.W. Chase, *Dr. Chase's Third Last and Complete Receipt Book and Household Physician,* 1903

Sponge Cake

Mix ¼ cup sugar and ½ cup flour, wet with a little cold milk, and stir into a pint of boiling milk. Cook until mixture is smooth and thick. Add a cup of butter. When well mixed, stir into the mixture the well beaten yolks of five eggs. Add the egg whites, beaten stiff. Bake in cups, shallow dishes, or paper cases in a hot oven. Place dish in a pan of hot water while in the oven. Serve with a creamy sauce.

—Mary Emma Wooley, inaugurated in 1901
as president of Mt. Holyoke College, Hadley, MA
Favorite Recipes of Famous 'Daughters'

Chocolate Tarts

Rub ½ cake of grated baker's chocolate smooth in 3 tablespoonsful milk, and heat to boiling over the fire, then stir in 1 tablespoonful corn-starch dissolved in water. Stir 5 minutes until well thickened; remove from the fire, and pour into a bowl. Beat the yolks of 4 eggs and the whites of 2 eggs with 4 tablespoonsful sugar, and when the chocolate mixture is almost cold, put all together with 2 teaspoonsful vanilla, 1 saltspoon salt, and ½ teaspoonful cinnamon. Stir until light. Bake in open shells of pastry. When done, cover with a méringue made of the whites of 2 eggs and 2 tablespoonsful sugar flavored with 1 teaspoonful lemon juice. Eat cold. These are nice for tea, baked in patty pans.

—*Common Sense in the Household,* 1871

New England Doughnuts

Sift 1 quart flour, ½ teaspoonful salt, ¼ teaspoonful grated nutmeg, and 3 teaspoonsful baking powder until mixed. Beat 2 eggs lightly with 1 tablespoonful Cottolene and 1 cup granulated sugar. Add 1 cup milk and the sifted flour. Some qualities of flour require a little more milk to make a soft dough. Roll out about ½ inch thick and cut with a ring cutter. When all are cut out, have ready the frying kettle with sufficient hot Cottolene to float the doughnuts while frying. Test with a piece of the dough. If it comes immediately to the sur-face, it is hot enough to begin frying. Cook about 3 minutes, turning frequently to keep them smooth and like balls. When taken from the fat, dust with powdered sugar and cinnamon.

—*Home Helps,* 1910

Indian Meal Pudding No. 2 (Grandmother's Rule)

Scald 1 quart milk. Mix 7 tablespoonsful Indian meal and 1 tablespoonful flour, and stir gradually into the scalded milk; add 1 cup molasses, ½ teaspoonful salt, and a little ginger. Butter pudding dish, pour in 1 pint of cold milk, then the above mixture, then another pint of cold milk, and put in the oven without stirring. Bake about three hours in a moderate oven.

—Mrs. Prentiss Webster, *Our Cook Book,* Lowell, MA, 1910

Oranges and Wafers

A new wrinkle at afternoon teas is the service of crackers or wafers spread with Sunkist orange. Put together sandwich fashion, and heat in the oven just long enough to allow the flavor and juice of the fruit to penetrate the cracker and soften it slightly.

—*Recipes for Dainty Dishes: Culinary Toilet, and Medicinal Hints,* ca. 1910s

Chocolate Blanc-Mange

Soak 1 package gelatin 2 hours in 3 pints milk and then put it in the double boiler. Scrape 11 ounces baker's chocolate fine, and put it in a small frying pan with 2 tablespoonsful sugar and 2 tablespoonsful boiling water. Stir this over a hot fire until smooth and glossy (it will take about 1 minute) and stir into the milk. Add 2 more tablespoonsful sugar and strain. Turn into molds, and set away to harden. This dish should be made at least 8 hours before being served. If you please, you can add 1 teaspoonful of vanilla extract.

—Earl S. Sloan, Boston, *Sloan's Cook Book and Advice to Housekeepers,* 1905

Victoria Fritters

Slice a loaf of baker's bread into pieces 1 inch thick; cut the slices in the center, trimming off the crust, and place them on a flat dish. Stir a quart of rich milk, 1 teaspoonful salt, and 8 beaten eggs together and pour over the bread several hours before dinner, that it may be equally moistened. Fry in hot butter a delicate brown, and eat with sweet wine sauce.

—C.I. Hood Apothecaries, Lowell, MA, *Hood's Cook Book Reprint Number One*, 1877

Mariners Tea Cake

Mix 1 pound flour, ½ pound butter, ¼ pound sugar, the yolks of 4 eggs, and the grated rind of one lemon, forming a paste. Roll ½ inch thick. Cut into 1 ½ inch squares. Varnish with egg yolk. Sprinkle with powdered sugar and bake on plates powdered with flour. This recipe was presented by Captain Sigsbee to the wife of Col. Clendarin, U.S.A., on board Battleship Maine, in Key West Harbor, January, 1898.

—Mrs. C.B. Abbott, Lowell, MA, *Our Cook Book,* 1910

Apricot Bombe

Drain a can of apricots and force them through a purée strainer. To the syrup add 1½ cups orange juice and ¼ cup lemon juice, a few salt grains, and apricot purée; then sweeten to taste. Freeze, using 3 parts finely crushed ice to 1 part rock salt. Line a melon mold with mixture, fill with praline ice cream. Cover ice cream with apricot mixture to overflow mold, adjust cover, pack in rock salt and ice, using equal parts, and let stand 3 hours.

—*Catering for Special Occasions,* 1911

Vanilla Ice Cream

The foundation given in this rule is suitable for all kinds of ice cream. Let a generous pint of milk come to a boil. Beat 1 cup of sugar, ½ scant cup of flour, and 2 eggs together, and stir into the boiling milk. Cook 20 minutes, stirring often. Set away to cool. When cool, add another cup of sugar, 1 tablespoonful vanilla extract, and 1 quart cream. Then put away to freeze.

—Earl S. Sloan, Boston, *Sloan's Cook Book and Advice to Housekeepers,* 1905

BEVERAGES

Cocoa

To 1 pint milk and 1 pint cold water add 3 tablespoonsful grated cocoa. Boil 15 or 20 minutes, milling or whipping. Sweeten to taste at the table. Some persons like a piece of orange peel boiled with it.

—*Housekeeping in Old Virginia*, 1879

How to Make Good Coffee

Mix 1 egg thoroughly with 2 heaping teaspoonful of coffee, put into the coffee pot, and pour on it 2 cups freshly boiling water. Boil 5 minutes, stir well with a fork, set on back of the stove to keep hot 5 minutes. Add ½ cup water, pour out a little coffee, to clean the grounds from the spout, and pour it back again. Then let stand 10 minutes and be careful not to shake the pot when serving. Serve with the best and richest cream, but, in the absence of this luxury, a good substitute may be found in boiled milk prepared as follows: place fresh new milk in a pan or pail, set where it will slowly simmer *but not boil* or reach the boiling point; stir frequently to keep the cream from separating and rising to the top; let simmer until it is rich, thick, and creamy.

—*Cereal Foods and How to Cook Them*, 1899

Whipped Syllabub

Take a lump of sugar and rub it on the outside of a lemon until colored, then put it into a pint of cream and sweeten to taste. Squeeze in the juice of a lemon, and add a glass of Sherry or Madeira. Mill to a froth, and take off the froth as it rises. Drain it well in a sieve, then fill half a glass with red wine, and pile up the froth as high as possible.

Prince Regent's Punch

Combine: 2 bottles claret, 1 bottle sherry, 1 bottle champagne, ½ dozen oranges sliced and seeded, 1 bottle good brandy, 1 bottle Jamaica rum, 3 quarts strong Oolong tea, 1 pint ripe strawberries, pineapple and enough sugar to make quite sweet. Stir and add a large piece of ice.

—Mrs. Prentiss Webster, Lowell, MA, *Our Cook Book*, 1910

Buttermilk

Farmers' families seldom appreciate what a delicious and healthful drink they have in homemade buttermilk. It was the fashionable drink in New York last summer, and brokers, bankers, and merchants indulged in it at three cents a glass, from street stands or wagons. Ice is not an essential where a beverage can be stood to cool in a porous earthen jar in a cold cellar or milkroom, such as belongs to every farmhouse.

—*Healy & Bigelow's New Cook Book*, 1890

Loving Cup

Melt and strain ¼ pound sugar, then place it in a cup holding 3 quarts, then add 1 bottle Scotch ale and 1 pint sherry; stir these well up. Just before serving, add a bottle of soda water, and on the froth, a little grated nutmeg. Place in a small piece of toasted bread and 4 slices of lemon, and take it to the table to drink immediately.

—*Peterson's Magazine*, March 1868

CHAPTER FOUR

COMPANY EXPECTED: SELECTED RECIPES FOR SPECIAL GATHERINGS

TEAS AND LUNCHEONS

For an afternoon tea a pretty way to serve sandwiches is to roll them and tie them with different colored ribbons; a stoned olive can be put inside of each one. Strawberries and cream, fancy cakes, Newport whips, iced tea, and seltzer lemonade are sufficient refreshments.

Russian Tea

Make same as Five O'Clock Tea (below), and allow ½ teaspoonful lemon juice and a thin slice of lemon from which seeds have been removed to each cup. Sweeten with cut sugar to suit individual taste. Many prefer the addition of 3 whole cloves or a candied cherry.

—*Catering for Special Occasions*, 1911

Five O'Clock Tea

Put 3 teaspoonsful tea in tea pot and pour on 2 cups boiling water. Let stand 3 minutes and strain into tea cups. Serve with cut sugar and cream.

—*Catering for Special Occasions*, 1911

Delicious Desserts for Spring Teas or Luncheons

SUNDAY   Lemon Jelly
Gold Cake
MONDAY   Floating Island
Chocolate Cake
TUESDAY   Sliced Oranges
Philadelphia Jumbles
WEDNESDAY   Boston Cream Cakes
THURSDAY   Currant and Raspberry Tarts with whipped cream
FRIDAY   Cup Custard
Fruit Cookies
SATURDAY   Baked Sweet Apples with whipped cream
Clove Cake

—*Dr. Price's Delicious Desserts*, 1904

The Tea Kettle...

*I*s as much an English institution as aristocracy or the Prayer Book; and when one wants to know exactly how tea should be made, one has only to ask how a fine old English housekeeper makes it. The first article of her faith is that the water must not merely be hot, not merely have boiled a few moments since, but be actually boiling at the moment it touches the tea... Tea making belongs to the drawing room, and high-born ladies preside at "the bubbling and loud-hissing urn," and see that all due rites and solemnities are properly performed— that the cups are hot, and that the infused tea waits the exact time before the libations commence.

—Harriet Beecher Stowe,
House and Home Papers, 1869

Austrian Coffee for Teas and Receptions

A coffee of the above name, sometimes served at teas and receptions, is a cold, strong coffee, creamed and sweetened. It is served in small glasses, with a tablespoonful of ice cream added in each glass after the coffee is put in

—*Mrs. Seely's Cook Book,* 1902

Gold or Silver Cake

Combine 2 cups of flour, ½ cup milk, ½ cup butter, 1 cup sugar, the yolks of 3 eggs, 1 teaspoonful soda and 2 teaspoonsful cream of tartar. Silver cake may be made the same as gold cake, only using a little more butter.

—*Sweet Home Cook Book,* 1888

Jam Jumble

Cream ½ cup butter; add 1 cup sugar gradually, 1 egg well beaten, ½ teaspoonful soda mixed with ½ cup sour milk, ¼

teaspoonful salt, and flour enough to make a soft dough. Chill, roll to ¼ inch in thickness, and shape, using a round cutter. On the centers of half the pieces put raspberry jam. Make three small openings in remaining halves (forming a triangle), using a thimble, and put pieces together. Press edges slightly, and bake in a rather hot oven, that jumbles may keep in good shape.

—*Catering for Special Occasions,* 1911

What Will You Have?

Thank you—a plate of any thing. Have you been to a country tea party before?

No, Never; I like it. Why do so many keep utter silence, though? A good many have only opened their mouths to eat, not to speak.

It is our way. Tomorrow they will speak fast enough; we shall be turned into hash.

Yet you invite such?

Oh, we must invite each other; we live so. Our events often come from these insignificant meetings.

Does that elderly lady enjoy herself, for instance? And he pointed to a silent spinster who held her third teacup, and who was looking everywhere with wide eyes.

Certainly. She has the pattern of all our dresses in her head, and can set forth our manners, and repeat all that has been said, at any moment from this table.

The bashful young man, who laughs so much, is he really entertained?

He is bashful here, but tomorrow, in the shops or loafing-places, he will be very bold and sneering in his remarks upon my attempt at society.

I see, a tea party is like others; or human nature in general.

—Elizabeth Sotddard, *"The Tea-Party,"* 1871

Floating Island

Take six eggs and separate them. Beat the yolks and stir into a quart of milk. Sweeten to taste and flavor with lemon or nutmeg. Put this in a dish and half immerse it in a saucepan of boiling water. Keep stirring it until the custard gets thick, which will be in about half an hour. Whip the whites of the eggs to a strong froth. When the custard is done, put it into a deep dish, and heap the frothed egg upon it. Serve this cold.

—Sweet Home Cook Book, 1888

Green Gooseberry Tart

Top and tail the gooseberries. Put into a porcelain kettle with enough water to prevent burning, and stew slowly until they break. Take them off, sweeten well, and set aside to cool. When cold, pour into pastry shells, and bake with a top crust of puff pastry. Brush all over with beaten egg while hot; set back in the over to glaze for 3 minutes. Eat cold.

—Common Sense in the Household, 187

Boston Cream Cakes

Put into a large-sized sauce pan ½ cup butter and one cup of hot water; set it on the fire. When the mixture begins to boil, turn in 1 pint sifted flour at once, beat and work it well with a vegetable masher until it is very smooth. Remove from the fire, and when cool enough add 5 eggs well beaten, first the yolks and then the whites, also ½ teaspoonful soda and 1 teaspoonful salt. Drop on buttered tins in large spoonfuls, about 2 inches apart. Bake in a quick oven about 15 minutes. When done and quite cold, open them on the side with a knife or scissors, and put in as much of the custard as possible.

Cream Custard for Filling

Mix 2 eggs, 3 tablespoons sifted flour or ½ cup corn-starch, and 1 cup sugar. Put 1 pint of milk over the fire in a double boiler. In ⅓ pint of

In a Moment…

Thirty people were round the well-lighted table, and in another were served with the edibles—biscuit, tongue, marmalade, delicious cake, fruited and plain, tarts, dishes of froth and amber, preserved fruits and cream; in short, all that the limits of Thornbury, distant from the city, allowed.

—Elizabeth Stoddard,
"The Tea-Party," 1871

milk, stir the sugar, flour, and beaten eggs. As soon as the milk looks like boiling, pour in the mixture, and stir briskly for 3 minutes, until it thickens. Then remove from the fire and add 1 teaspoonful of butter. When cool, flavor with vanilla or lemon, and fill your cakes.

—*White House Cook Book*, 1887

Cream Scones

Sift 2 cups flour, 3 teaspoonsful baking powder, and 1 teaspoonful salt together. Work in 4 tablespoons of butter with your fingertips. Mix 2 well beaten eggs and ⅓ cup thin cream, then stir into flour. Knead and roll into sheet ¾ inch thick. Cut into diamond shape, prick, brush with slightly-beaten white of egg, and sprinkle with sugar. Bake in a hot oven for 15 minutes.

—Miss J.H. Earl, Lowell, MA, *Our Cook Book*, 1910

Honor Sandwiches for St. Valentine's Tea

Cut white bread in ¼ inch slices, and shape with heart cutter. Spread with pimento butter, put together in pairs, and arrange on a fancy plate covered with a doily.

Pimento butter—Cream 2 tablespoonsful butter, add one canned pimento forced through a sieve, and work until thoroughly blended. Then season with salt.

—*Catering for Special Occasions*, 1911

Watercress Sandwiches

Wash well some watercress, and then dry them in a cloth, pressing out every atom of moisture, as far as possible; then mix with the cresses hard boiled eggs chopped fine and seasoned with salt and pepper. Have a stale loaf and some fresh butter, and with a sharp knife, cut as many thin slices as will be required for two dozen sandwiches. Then cut the cress into small pieces, removing the stems; place it between each slice of bread and butter, with a slight sprinkling of lemon juice. Press down the slices hard, and cut them sharply on a board into small squares, leaving no crust.

—White House Cook Book, 1887

Sandwich Fillings for Picnics and Daytime Gatherings

- ☞ Vegetable: 1 ounce rhubarb juice, 1 ounce peanuts, 1 ounce carrots, and 1 ounce celery.
- ☞ Cottage cheese and chopped dates.
- ☞ Grated cheese and minced onion.
- ☞ Chopped nuts and raisins: 1 ½ cup seeded raisins and ½ cup chopped nuts, blended with ½ lemon juice.
- ☞ Lettuce, cream cheese, and chopped olives.
- ☞ Equal parts dates, peanut butter, and cream cheese.
- ☞ Cottage cheese and grated nuts, moistened with cream.
- ☞ Equal parts chopped nuts and chopped olives.
- ☞ Apples and cream cheese: peel and grate 1 tart apple; mix ½ cup cream cheese and 1 tablespoonful cream. Add apple and mix.
- ☞ Flaked peanuts moistened with lemon juice and honey.
- ☞ Lettuce and peanut butter mixed with lemon juice. Put peanut butter mixture on buttered bread and lay on lettuce leaves.
- ☞ Equal parts macerated dates and grated American cheese.

—International Health Resort Recipes, ca. 1900s

OTHER OCCASIONS

Pumpkin Pie

Stew a kettle full of pumpkin and press it through a colander. For 1 quart of the stewed pumpkin, use about 1 pint or a little more of sweet milk, 2 cups of sugar, 3 eggs and 1 teaspoonful of ginger; bake in a crust in a deep pie plate.

—A.W. Chase, *Dr. Chase's Third Last and Complete Receipt Book and Household Physician*, 1903

Roast Goose

Boil 6 potatoes; pare them, then mash them fine and light. Combine with 1 tablespoonful each salt and pepper, a teaspoonful of sage, and 2 tablespoonsful each onion juice and butter.

—Earl S. Sloan, Boston, *Sloan's Cook Book and Advice to Housekeepers*, 1905

Eggnog

Beat the yolks and whites of the eggs separately; one for each person is sufficient. Mix the sugar and brandy with the yolks, a wineglassful to each egg is the proportion. Then pour in sufficient cream to dilute, and lastly, mix with the whipped whites and pour into a punch-bowl.

—*Godey's Lady's Book*, December 1896

Child's Christmas Cake

Beat 3 eggs and then gradually beat in 1½ cups sugar; add ½ teaspoonful lemon extract, then 1½ cups flour, which has been sifted with ¼ teaspoonful salt, ¾ level teaspoonful soda, and 1½ teaspoonsful cream tartar or 2½ teaspoonsful baking powder. When thoroughly mixed, beat in ¾ cup hot milk. Bake in a well buttered tube pan for half an hour.

—Mrs. F.C. Church, Lowell, MA, *Our Cook Book,* 1910

Menu for Christmas Dinner

Consommé   Bread Sticks
Olives   Celery   Salted Pecans
Roast Goose   Potato Stuffing   Apple Sauce
Duchess Potatoes   Cream of Lima Beans
Chicken Croquettes with Green Peas
Dressed Lettuce with Cheese Straws
English Plum Pudding   Brandy Sauce
Frozen Pudding   Assorted Cake   Bonbons
Crackers   Cheese   Café Noir

—*Boston Cooking-School Cook Book,* 1896

Fourth of July Punch

Boil 1 cup sugar and ½ cup water five minutes; add juice from 2 lemons and 2 oranges as well as 1 can sliced pineapple cut in pieces, ½ cup raspberry syrup, ¼ cup brandy, 1 pint bottle Moselle wine, and 1 pint bottle Apollinaris. Pour over a cake of ice.

—*Catering for Special Occasions*, 1911

Priscilla Popped Corn for Halloween

Put 2 tablespoons butter in saucepan, and when melted add 2 cups brown sugar, ½ teaspoonful salt, and ½ cup water. Bring to boiling point and let boil 16 minutes. Pour over 3 quarts popped corn, and stir until every kernel is well coated with mixture.

—*Catering for Special Occasions*, 1911

Wedding Cake

Use 50 eggs, 5 pounds each sugar, flour, and butter; 15 pounds raisins, 3 pounds citron, 10 pounds currants, 1 pint brandy, ¼ ounce cloves, 1 ounce cinnamon. 4 ounces mace, and 4 ounces nutmeg. This makes 44½ pounds, and keeps 20 years.

—*Centennial Buckeye Cookbook*, 1876

Maids of Honor (for showers)

Put both 1 cup sweet and 1 cup sour milk together in a vessel, which is set in another, and let it become sufficiently heated to set the curd. Then strain off the milk, rub the curd through a strainer, add 1 tablespoon butter to the curd, 1 slight cup white powdered sugar, the well beaten yolks of 5 eggs, and the juice and rind of the lemon. Line the little pans with the richest of puff pastry, and fill with the mixture. Bake until firm in the center, from 10 to 16 minutes.

—*White House Cook Book*, 1887

PART FIVE

The Keeper of the Family

CHAPTER ONE

THE MOTHER: GUIDELINES FOR HER CHILDREN'S WELL-BEING

Each wisely brought-up and well-educated child is the best of all investments of a parent's wealth of money, affection, and effort.

Rules for a Mother to Live By

DO NOT LET SERVANTS STAND IN YOUR PLACE. That children are so much left to the care of servants in so many families of the middle classes is, perhaps, in many cases unavoidable. Nevertheless, it is a great evil. It has been observed that children who are attended to by their mother, who are undressed and put to bed by her, who open their eyes in the morning to behold her cheerful eyes and loving looks, who by her are dressed and kept under her judicious care throughout the day are, as a rule, far more good-tempered, healthy, and intelligent than such as are left almost wholly to the care of servants.

'TIS TRUE, AN ANGEL MIGHT SHRINK FROM THE RESPONSIBILITIES OF A MOTHER. The watch must not for an instant be relaxed; the scales of justice must always be nicely balanced; the hasty word that the over-tasked spirit sends to the lip must die there ere it is uttered.

The timid and sensitive child must have a word of encouragement in season, and the forward and presuming must be checked with gentle firmness. And all when the exhausted frame sinks with ceaseless vigils, and the thousand petty interruptions and unlooked-for annoyances of every hour almost set at defiance any attempt at system. For all these duties faithfully performed, a mother's reward is in secret.

Rules for Their Sleep

MOTHER, YOU MUST PUT HIM TO BED. There are some mothers who think it a self-denial to leave the parlors, firesides, or work to put their little children to bed. They think that the nurse could do it just as well, that it is of no consequence who hears the children say their prayers. But of this all mothers may be assured, that the last words at night are of great importance, even to the babies of the flock; the very tones of the voice they last listened to make an impression on their sensitive organizations. Mother, do not think the time and strength wasted which you spend in reviewing the day with your little boy or girl. It has had its disappointments and trials as well as its play and pleasures; it is ready to throw its arms around your neck and take its goodnight kiss.

PROVIDE SEPARATE SLEEPING ENCLOSURES. Where should the infant sleep? Never in bed between the parents. When placed between the parents, the infant must constantly inhale the poisonous emanations from the bodies of two adults. It should sleep by the side of the mother's bed in a crib.

DON'T USE THE OLD-FASHIONED CRADLE. The emanations from the sleeper's lungs and skin should be allowed to escape freely. This is impossible in a close, deep cradle. The crib, with the skeleton sides, is just the thing. If his head is too high at night, round shoulders will result; uneven shoulders result from allowing a child to sleep continually on one side.

USE PROPER BEDDING. The best bed at all seasons of the year is one of oat straw. This is light and soft. It is better than hair, because the

[163]

straw can often be changed and the tick washed. In cold weather, a thick woolen blanket should be doubled and spread over the straw bed to increase the warmth. For covering the little sleeper, woolen blankets should alone be used.

MAKE CLOTHES FOR SLEEPING. Children should not wear the same garment next to the skin at night which they have worn through the day. If the nightgown is worn more than one night without going to the wash-room, it should be hung up to be thoroughly aired during the day, and if possible in the sun.

AVOID EXCESSIVE EVENING STIMULATION. Certainly it would be unwise to excite young children by too much conversation with them just before putting them to bed. All study should be forbidden in the evening for children who have difficulty going to sleep. Every mother who carefully studies the temperament of her children will know how to manage them in this respect.

SEND HIM TO BED HAPPY. Always see for yourself that his last waking thoughts are pleasant, that he shuts his eyes at peace with the world and in love with you. Whatever cares may trouble your mind, give the dear child a warm good-night kiss as it goes to its pillow. The memory of this, in the stormy years which may be in store for the little one, will be like Bethlehem's star to the bewildered shepherds, and welling up in the heart will rise the thought: "My father, my mother loved me!"

SOOTHE THE CHILD WHO CANNOT SLEEP. Nervous children who toss and turn and cry out that they cannot go to sleep may sometimes be quieted by having their feet rubbed vigorously with a flesh brush. A warm bath will sometimes be effectual, but generally it does not conduce to quiet so much as waken. After adjusting the physical appliances which tend to sleep, tell him to picture himself a little winding brook off in the deep woods carrying upon it a leaf or a chip.

LET THEM WAKE OF THEMSELVES. Never wake up young children of a morning. It is a barbarity.

- Graham hasty pudding.
- The inner part of a well-roasted apple.
- In their season, ripe peaches.

MOTHER, PROTECT HIM. Hundreds of infants have been killed by the mistakes of parents in giving them improper foods. Thus, take care to avoid:

- Food prepared for other members of the family, as the table foods may be poisonous to the infant.
- Skin of an apple, which is as bad for him as a bit of your kid gloves would be, and the skin of a grape is more indigestible than sole-leather.
- Raisins—"skins and all"—which are unfit for anybody to eat and poisonous for baby.

VER GIVE A CHILD UNDER TWO YEARS OF AGE THESE FOODS:

Ham, bacon, or pork in any other form.

Cabbage, pickles, or other succulent vegetables.

Coffee, tea, beer, wine, cider, or any other liquor of any kind.

Bananas, berries, or other fruit except prune juice.

Pastries or preserves.

ghts on Their Dress (and Yours)

LITTLE GIRLS AS COMFORTABLY AS BOYS. Let parents heed monitions and warnings, and put them into immediate prac-
 the writer not a whit too sharply: On cold, blowy days, I am
 see the efforts of foolish parents to freeze their little girls. It
 rage. The poor little shivering things are sent out into the
 th their heads comfortably protected and thick shawls
 eir shoulders, which comparatively need no protection,
 standing out at an angle of forty-five degrees and their
 drum-stick legs as unprotected from the blasts as the legs

Goodnight Prayer

"Father, now the day is past, on thy child thy blessing cast;
Near my pillow hand in hand, keep thy guardian angel band;
And throughout the darkening night, bless me with a cheerful light.
Let me rise at morn again, free from every care and pain;
Pressing through life's thorny way, keep me, Father, day by day."

Rules for Their Diets

Ahe quality of food intended for little children should be carefully studied, as the firmness of their flesh and the hardness of their bones is so dependent upon it.

FEED THEIR HUNGER. When children get hungry more often than the ocurrence of the regular family meals, they should be supplied with a light repast of digestible character. If a child is hungry, it cannot be well or happy, and the rapid growth of youth causes a constant demand to be made upon the vitality supplied to the system by food.

PARENTS, MONITOR THEIR INTAKE. Every abnormal appetite should be modified by judicious control on the part of the parents or nurse if the child is to receive the care its helpless condition imposes upon its natural protectors. When children show any marked preference for special foods, care should be taken to modify their tastes.

SERVE EACH MEAL THUS:

❧ The breakfast should be early and plentiful.

❧ Mid-day dinners should he varied and always hot—indeed, all food is most digestible when warm—and composed of some plain meat dish, at least two vegetables, and a simple pudding. Soup is invaluable for children, but it must be plain.

❧ The supper, given about two hours before retiring, should be light and nutritious and may include warm bread and milk, any form of porridge and milk, custard, bread and butter, simple stewed fruits, and either cool water or cocoa as a beverage.

Particular Rules for Feeding Little Ones Under Three

These outlines will serve to guard those having the care of children from making the mistakes which too often entail a life of weakness or suffering as the consequence equally of injudicious indulgence and of neglect of the most ordinary rules of health.

KEEP WATCH OVER THE COOKING. Unless you have a nurse whom you know for yourself to be faithful and experienced, always superintend the cooking of baby's food.

LET THE GROWTH OF HIS TEETH GUIDE YOU. Nature's supply is seldom in advance of the demand. If he did not need what the teeth are

---

☞

The Care of a Child

 Nursing women should not give way to temper. Anger, anxiety, suspense, fear, terror, and undue conditions of any kind will turn the milk to poison.

Gradual weaning is much better than the sudden removal of the child from the breast... A child should not be weaned in the hot months.

—Earl S. Sloan, *Sloan's Cook Book and Advice to Houseekeepers,* 1905

---

designed to chew, you may be sure they would not be given him. T cutting of the eighth incisors or front teeth, which occurs usually d ing the twelfth month, may be taken as nature's indication that child requires other food than milk. Rare beef and well-boiled ton, tender roast, or boiled chicken and turkey are safe. Wit fried meats of every description. Do not let him touch veal or any shape. Mince the meat very finely to save his digestive ap all unnecessary work.

*The Well Being of Our Nation's Yo
Rests with Their Mothers*

GIVE TO HIM THESE FOODS:

❋ Mealy old potatoes—never new or wax

❋ Young onions, boiled in two waters.

❋ Fresh asparagus, green peas, and dry fice for vegetables.

❋ Rice and hominy, of course.

GIVE HIM THESE, ONCE IN A WHILE, FO

▦ A simple custard.

▦ A taste of homemade ice cream

Thou

DRESS
these a
tice. Say
pained t
is an out
streets w
around t
their skirt
poor little

of a turkey hanging in a meat stall. And thus we pack off these little girls to school, with their big heads to be crammed full of learning, at the expense of their legs, which, at a tender age, are of more importance than their heads.

Faculty

"I had, in no mean degree, the talent that, in our New England parlance, is called 'faculty.' With me it was a tolerable substitute for the wealth that fortune had denied... My parents had been 'principaled,' as Yankees say, against debts, and the inheritance of the principle was, with me, a stimulus to 'faculty.'

My husband's every-day vests were invariably made of the odds and ends left from other garments, and the linings of his study-gowns were like the Scriptural coat of Joseph in the variety of colors brought together. Pantaloons whose legs had been amputated, and sewed on so as to bring the darned knees behind, whose worn-out seats had been carefully cut out and undarned cloth substituted, but whose whole appearance was, nevertheless, respectable, were considered good enough for home wear, and stockings that had been heeled and toed and re-footed over and over, kept [his] clerical feet warm when plodding through the snows of Winter. Our whole wardrobe was in a perpetual struggle to be created anew. Only the Sunday suit... was exempt from renovation."

—H.C. Gardner, *How My Old Silk Was Made Over,* 1876

PROTECT THEIR ARMS AND SHOULDERS. If the mother desires to exhibit her darling's beautiful skin, let her cut out a bit of the dress upon its chest; when the neighbors come in, let her show the skin thus exposed to the company. If you would save a child from croup, pneumonia, and a score of other grave affections, keep its arms warm.

Do not contract the waists of your little girls. Thousands of women are rendered unfit for marriage and motherhood by what they suffer as the result of tight lacing—not but what there are scores of corset-wearing mothers, but point out to me one healthy one out of each score, and I'll show you nineteen prematurely wrinkled and wan, fretful, and ailing women to offset your one. Mothers, it is your bounden duty to give your girls the best health possible, and as you love them, shield them from the misery and suffering which has marred your own life. Do not kill them with foolish kindness as your mothers did you; fill their bodies with sound organs.

Mind your own dress for them. Many a good, kind, loving mother has made her son or her daughter extremely unhappy by appearing not as well dressed, or not as considerate of the ways of the world as her children have a right to expect. We are told in the good book about respect due to our parents, but you and I and the other woman have a right to respect our children, and not to cause them to be mortified by our personal appearance. This may sound a little cruel, but I am sure you will see its truth if you will only remember the times when you have seen your boy's or your girl's face flush because "mother didn't look like the other ladies."

Some Advice for Their Playtime

Amuse the baby simply. One mother used to give her baby a wide-mouthed bottle and a box of beans, and he would amuse himself for a long time dropping them one by one into the bottle. Another amusement for a child just old enough to stand beside a chair is to give him a lead pencil and let him poke holes through a paper as it lies across a cane-seated chair. Simple as was the device, it helped the mother to "make time" and so the end desired was gained.

Let them make their own. Playthings that the children make for themselves are a great deal better than those which are bought for them. A little girl had better fashion her cups and saucers of acorns than to have a set of earthen ones supplied. A boy takes ten times more pleasure in a little wooden cart he has pegged together than he would in a painted and gilded carriage bought from the toy-shop.

MAKE HER A DOLL. For the wee little girl, make a nice rag doll. It will please her as well as a boughten one, and besides, that sort of a dollie can be handled ever so roughly without any danger of breaking its neck or limbs.

SEND THEM OUT. The truth is that "all out doors," as the phrae is, is the only proper apartment for them. Nothing can make up for it—for the gleeful delight of picking shells upon the sea-shore, or paddling with dimpled feet in the foam of the waves, or plucking a handsful of flowers wheresoever it chooses to stray, or looking at the animal creation, every one of which, from a caterpillar to an ox, is a marvel and wonder compared to which a toy-shop is of no interest whatever. We are taking it for granted that such a child is neither fettered by fine clothes or tyrannized over by a stupid, ignorant, selfish nurse.

TAKE YOUR BABY OUT, TOO. A baby can no more flourish in the dark than a flower. Like the flower, it needs sunshine, and should, like it, have the direct rays from the sun. Do not fear its eyes will be injured if the sun shine in its face, and when you take it out to ride, unless the sun is coming down very strong, do not cover up its face with the carriage top.

ENCOURAGE FRIENDSHIPS. Children, to be truly happy, must have the companionship of other children. Unless a child's companions are known to be really objectionable, the evil of no companionship is apt to be greater than the risk run in letting him play with his mates.

MAKE FUN IN THE WORK OF THE HOME. A toy flatiron is sold that is not only useful in the hands of a child for ironing dolls' clothes but also as a lesson in domestic economy.

LET THEM MAKE THEIR OWN HOME. Manufacturing some sort of a "little house," furnishing it, and living in it, is an occupation which children love, to which they are devoted for weeks, which they utterly forget, and to which they fondly return.

For a little lady of two-and-a-half years
this will do:

She had picked up a cane in the corner of the room and was
playing with it—a place stick bent at the end. Papa asked,
"What are you doing with the cane?"

"It isn't a cane."

"What is it, then?"

"It's an umbrella without any clothes on."

—*Harper's New Monthly Magazine*, 1868

GARDEN WITH THEM. Encourage the children in gardening by giving them a corner "all for their own" and some seeds to put in it. Show
them how to make beds and take care of them. Tell them how flowers
grow and encourage them to watch and study them in their develop-
ment. Such employment will keep them out of a great deal of mis-
chief. There can be no safer companions than flowers.

CHAPTER TWO

---

*T*HE INSTRUCTRESS: GUIDELINES FOR REARING LITTLE LADIES AND GENTLEMEN

As Children

The Parental Example

If parents realized how great was their responsibility, how closely they were watched and copied, they would place a perpetual guard upon their lips and manners.

BE WHAT YOU WOULD HAVE THEM BECOME. Mother, Father, be what the children ought to be. Do what the children ought to do. Avoid what they should avoid. Think well that those by whom you are surrounded are often only the reflection of yourself. Are any among them defective? Examine what you are yourself, what you avoid—in a word, your whole conduct. Do you discover in yourself defects, sins, wandering? Begin by improving yourself and seek afterward to improve your children.

ASSURE THAT YOUR HUSBAND IS WITH THEM. The father who plunges into business so deeply that he has no leisure for domestic pleasures and whose only intercourse with his children consists in a brief word of authority or a surly lamentation over their intolerable expensiveness is to be both pitied and blamed.

BE HONEST, BE RIGHT. Let there be no deception, no trickery for the keen eye of childhood to detect. Rule your own spirit and wear an unruffled brow lest the smiling cherub on her knee catch your angry frown. Never stoop to pander with expediency. If a question of right or wrong comes up for decision, meet it squarely. Let your children feel that mother and father are always found on the side of the right, and not policy.

The Proper Use of Praise and Punishment

There are two great motives influencing human action—hope and fear. Both of these are at times necessary. But who would not prefer to have her child influenced to good conduct by a desire of pleasing rather than by the fear of offending?

UNDERSTAND AND REASON WITH THEM. Children are very delicate instruments. Men play upon them as if they were tough as drums and, like drums, made for beating. Do not terrorize them, but reason gently and plainly with them. One in sympathy with their little souls will lead them along safely amid temptations to falsehood.

APPRECIATE, RESPECT, AND TRUST THEM. Show the young people of your household that you respect their efforts and aid them with your riper judgment, and they will strive harder to be worthy of the trust you put in them. As flowers cannot grow without sunlight, neither can the young thrive unless they are treated with consideration and assistance.

PRAISE THEM. Parents who never have a word of praise for their children, who deny a bit of approval or a welcoming smile to their own—although they are generous enough with both to strangers—do not know what they are doing. They are chilling the warmest feelings of the heart. They are withering the bright blossoms of love and confidence which cannot live without careful nurture.

Keep Calm

"I am sick, just now, of this good housekeeping—excellent system, perfect regularity—living in a smooth, round nutshell, that never had any kernel."

"That will do for now; this is no occasion for such behavior. The parlor needs dusting; I wish you would shake out all the mats on the centre-table and stands. Keep calm, Clara."

—Elizabeth Stoddard, "The Tea-Party," 1871

SPEAK GENTLY. I know some houses in which sharp, angry tones resound from morning till night, and the influence is as contagious as measles and much more to be dreaded in a household. The children catch it and it lasts for life—an incurable disease.

Guiding Their Behavior as Children

Certain people to sneer at the word "etiquette" and claim that it merely means a foolish pandering to frivolous customs which in themselves have no meaning or use. This is a misapprehension which a little thoughtful consideration will remove. A knowledge of etiquette may be said to be an important part of good breeding.

TEACH THEM THESE RULES FOR DEPORTMENT:

⊛ *Respect for others.* Children can be trained to reciprocate courtesies and to behave politely everywhere without making prim little martinets of them. Teach them to respect each other's rights—to enjoy their merry romp and innocent fun without hurting each other's feelings or playing upon some weakness.

⊛ *Obedience.* Let us acknowledge the habit of obedience to be the primary virtue. The first lesson a child should be taught is filial respect and a deferent yielding of its own wishes to those of its parents. This does not imply a slavish submission or a crushing-out of individuality. It means that the tie between parent and child should be so strong and the confidence so great that there would be no chance for the clashing of will.

* *Courtesy.* Children must not be allowed to have two sets of manners, one for home use and the other for company. They can be taught to exercise gentle manners at home, to be thoughtful of the comfort of every member of the family, and to be guilty of no act that they would blush for were other eyes upon them. Then they will become real gentlemen or ladies.

Letter from the Wife of a Settler Who Cannot Settle

Dear Elizabeth,

My dear Simson has concluded to settle in America, and we are now on our way thither, on board of the Great Western . . . Simson, dear fellow, is full of plans and rural felicity, and we clear a farm, erect our buildings, and grow rich every day, sometimes in one place and sometimes in another, but have not yet made up our minds where.

New England is a well-regulated country . . . having more educated men and accomplished women in it than any other place; but they all talk gibberish, and I hardly feel equal to learning a foreign language, now that I have this little angel to watch over and take care of, and do not like to live among a people whom I do not understand. Besides, I couldn't think of poor little Bob giving up his English altogether, and talking nothing but Yankee Doodle.

—Thomas Haliburton, *The Letter-Bag of the Great Western,* 1873

Teaching Table Manners

Some little folks are not polite at their meals. The following standards are so simple, practical, comprehensive, and directly to the point, we take pleasure in placing them conspicuously before our readers. They will bear memorizing.

In silence I must take my seat;
And give God thanks before I eat;
Must for my food in patience wait
Till I am asked to hand my plate;
I must not scold, nor whine, nor pout,
Nor move my chair or plate about;
With knife, or fork, or napkin ring,
I must not play—nor must I sing;
I must not speak a useless word;
For children must be seen—not heard;
I must not talk about my food,
Nor fret if I don't think it good;
My mouth, with food I must not crowd,
Nor while I'm eating speak aloud;
Must turn my head to cough or sneeze,
And when I ask, say, "If you please;"
The tablecloth I must not spoil,
Nor with my food my fingers soil;
I must keep my seat when I am done,
Nor round the table sport or run;
When told to rise, then I must put
My chair away with noiseless foot,
And lift my heart to God above,
In praise for all his wondrous love.

—Children's Repository 1865

* *Respect for elders.* Teach them to be deferent to those who are their superiors in age and position. "Young America" has the idea that it is a proof of independence and manliness to speak flippantly and sneeringly of parents or guardians, referring to them as "the governor," "the old lady," or "the old party." There is no greater mistake made, and the listeners who may smile at such "wit" will just as surely censure for such coarseness and disrespect.

* *Order.* Teach them to have certain places for their clothes, toys, tools, and books; and when they are done using them, to put them in their place. Cultivate this habit, and they will grow into neat, orderly ladies and gentlemen, the pride of their mothers, welcome in every home which they visit.

* *Fairness.* Teach them to be fair in play, and not to cheat. This may be a hard lesson to learn, but it is one of the grandest.

* *Silence.* It is very rude for children to ask direct questions, such as "Where are you going?" or "What have you got in that package?" In fact, they should not show curiosity about other people's affairs.

* *Modesty.* Modesty among boys and girls is as highly appreciated as among grown people, and a young person who ventures to think himself a little better than his associates can hardly help carrying the thought into action. By such conduct he makes himself exceedingly disagreeable.

* *Succinctness.* If they have occasion to enter a place of business, train your children to state what they want and then retire as quickly as possible. They have no right to encroach upon the time of a man of business.

As Young Men and Women

Guiding Their Behavior Outside the House

If you hope for your children that they will choose and marry a partner as fine as they, you will instruct them how to properly conduct themselves when in public and when acquainting themselves with the opposite sex.

GENTLEMEN, AWAIT YOUR INVITATION. A gentleman cannot consider himself privileged to call upon a lady upon the strength of an introduction alone. He may desire very much to do so but waits to be invited. If the invitation does not come and he is anxious to prosecute the acquaintance, he may leave his card at her residence. If he is acceptable, the young lady's mother will send him an invitation to visit the family or ask his presence at some entertainment to be given at their home. After that, it is plain sailing, and the gentleman can feel that he has a right to call occasionally.

GENTLEMEN, CARRY YOUR CARDS. On making a first call a gentleman must have a card for each lady of the household. When there are several sisters in a family and the mother is living, two cards will answer—one for the mother and one for the daughters.

IT IS INAPPROPRIATE FOR A YOUNG LADY TO:

- Offer her hand with the same freedom as does a married or an elderly lady; the hand should never be extended to those who are not intimate friends.
- Permit one of the opposite sex to address her in a slangy fashion, touch her on the shoulder, or call her by her first name before strangers.
- Flirt on the street.
- Allow a stranger to make her acquaintance.
- Hear a rude remark or see an impertinent glance—she should be incapable of appearing to think it possible that they could be intended for her.
- Strike a gentleman with her handkerchief or tap him with her fan.

BEWARE GIVING INAPPROPRIATE GIFTS. The only gifts which should pass between ladies and gentlemen who are not relatives are books, flowers, music, and confectionery. Flowers are the most unobjectionable and welcome of gifts. There is a delicacy in selecting an offering, whether of gratitude, kindness, or affection that sometimes puzzles a considerate mind, but where any such hesitancy occurs, we can turn to flowers with complacency.

LADIES, WHILE OUT:

❧ Walk in an easy, unassuming manner, neither looking to the right or to the left, nor walking too quickly. If anything in a store window attracts her notice, she can stop and examine it with propriety and then resume her walk. In bowing on the street, a lady must merely incline her head gracefully and not her body. But she should always smile pleasantly. It lights up the features and adds a refreshing warmth to the greeting. Ladies do not chew gum on the streets.

Boston Women

*I*t has been remarked by an old bachelor who professes to be particularly astute in knowledge of the female character, that an American girl loves with her eyes, an English girl with her arms, a French girl with her lips, and Italian and Spanish girls with all three. A Boston woman capitulates in three months, a New York woman in two, and a New Orleans woman in one. Causes are partly climatic and constitutional and partly a few words from the old folks in the backroom.

—"Editor's Drawer," *Harper's New Monthly Magazine,* 1868

❧ In passing people on the walk, turn to the right. Do not join forces with three or four others and take up the entire pathway, compelling everyone to turn out for you. Walk in couples when there are several friends in your party. Do not pass between two persons who are talking together.

❧ Do not introduce people in a public conveyance. It draws attention to a person and makes him unpleasantly conspicuous.

❧ Whispering during a lecture is impudent, and interrupting a speaker is insulting.

❧ Do not seize hold of a piece of goods that another customer is examining, but wait until she has either made a purchase or passed it by.

❧ Do not pass in or out of the general entrance of a hotel but by the ladies' entrance only.

❧ Feel free to make yourself agreeable to fellow passengers, if the journey be long, without being misconstrued, but an acquaintance begun on a railway train should end there.

Gentlemen, while out:

❧ Bow to all you meet. Bow to the old, the young, the rich, the poor, to our friends, and to those to whom you are indifferent. Each one of these salutes can be shaded so nicely that, to an observant eye, they have a distinct significance of their own. With friends of your own sex, a bow and a friendly word in passing are sufficient.

❧ Refrain, at the theatre, from loud thumping with canes and umbrellas in demonstration of applause; it is voted decidedly rude. Clapping the hands is quite as efficient and neither raises a dust to soil the dresses of the ladies nor a hubbub enough to deafen them.

❧ Greet ladies only if prompted. A lady in the street, boulevard, or park may not be saluted by a gentleman unless he has received a slight bow from her. He may then raise his hat with the hand farthest from the person saluted, bow respectfully and pass on, not under any consideration pausing to speak unless the lady pauses in her promenade. If the lady friend is with another lady, he should include her in the salutation even though he is unacquainted with her; a gentleman must not presume upon such a chance introduction to a lady to call at her house or to walk with her when he meets her again.

❧ It is not obligatory to remove your glove when shaking hands with a lady. If you choose, you can say, "Excuse my glove," or observe a silence concerning it. A gentleman should not shake a lady's hand so violently as to annoy her, nor press it with such force that you will hurt her fingers.

Walk with discretion. Gentlemen will not swing their arms nor sway their bodies in an ungainly manner when walking; ladies are never guilty of any such ungraceful action and need no counsel in that respect. A gentleman never swaggers along the street shouting and laughing with his companions, his hat on one side, a cigar between his fingers, or switching a cane to the danger or discomfort of passers-by.

 Do not smoke while walking with a lady, not even if she politely fibs by saying it is not offensive to her; in fact, he should not smoke where ladies are under any circumstances. If smoking and passes a lady quite near, remove the cigar from your mouth. Should a lady accost you on the street when you are smoking, you should at once extinguish his cigar and decline politely but firmly to resume it. Although there is no intentional disrespect in smoking, the act under such circumstances conveys to other persons the idea of slight regard for the lady.

 If meeting a lady friend with whom you wish to converse, do not make her stand in the street, but walk with her a short distance until you have said what you desired to and leave her with a courteous bow.

 Refrain from whistles; whistling is exceedingly impertinent.

 In passing through a door, the gentleman holds it open for the

---

Old Colony Railroad...

Comprises 300 miles of line, extending from Boston, the metropolis of New England, to Newport, R.I., and to all the principal cities, towns, and villages of Southeastern Massachusetts, and, by its connecting lines of steamboats, forming the most desirable and popular route between New York and Boston, and the famous summer resorts of the beautiful islands of Nantucket and Martha's Vineyard.

—Thomas Haliburton, *The Old Colony Railroad: Its Connections, Popular Resorts, and Fashionable Watering-Places*, 1875 lady, even though he never saw her before. He also precedes the lady in ascending stairs and allows her to precede him in descending.

Guidelines for Young Ladies when Escorted

SET THE COURSE AND PACE. When walking with a lady, the gentleman should find out before they start if she has any preference as to the route. He should accommodate himself to her pace.

LADIES, CARRY SOME ARTICLES. The parasol, when that is necessary as a sun shade, must not be borne by the gentleman unless because of sickness or old age the lady requires peculiar assistance. A lady at a ball should not burden a gentleman with her gloves, fan, and bouquet to hold while she dances, unless he is her husband or brother.

ALLOW THE ESCORT TO ATTEND ALL WHILE TRAVELING. When traveling with an escort, a lady should not concern herself with any of the details of her trip. It is presumed that he knows more about traveling than she does, and it will annoy him to be continually asked about the safety of baggage, whether they are on the right train, and numberless other fussy questions that would scarcely be excusable in children. The lady or her relatives should supply the escort with sufficient money to defray all her expenses. Some prefer to have the gentleman attend to these matters and settle the account at the end of the journey, but a strict record of all the items should be kept in this case.

LEARN THE ART OF THE HORSEBACK MOUNT. It is quite an art to help a lady to mount horseback. She should place her left foot in one of his hands, with her left hand upon his shoulder and her right hand on the pommel of the saddle. Then at a given word, she springs up, the gentleman at the same time raising his hand so that he assists her into the saddle. In riding, he should always keep on her right side.

GENTLEMEN, HOLD THE UMBRELLA OVER THE LADY. A gentleman should not monopolize the umbrella when with two ladies in a rainstorm but should take the outside, holding it over both.

REST IF FATIGUED. During a walk in the country, ascending a hill, or walking on the bank of a stream, if the lady is fatigued and sits upon the ground, the gentleman does not seat himself by her but remains standing until she is rested sufficiently to proceed.

ACCEPT AID. A lady may accept the assistance of a strange gentleman in crossing a muddy or crowded street; such attentions should be accepted in the spirit in which they are offered and acknowledged with thanks.

Guidelines for Young Gentlemen when Escorting

SET THE PATH. Gentlemen walking with a lady or with a gentleman venerable for years, attainments, or office will give the inner path to the person escorted, unless the outer portion of the walk is safer. The concession will be made without remark, and the lady will assume whenever the gentleman changes his position that there is a sufficient reason for moving from one side to the other.

OFFER ARM WITH DISCRETION. A gentleman, when walking with a lady in the daytime, does not offer her his arm, unless she is old or ill or he does so for the purpose of protecting her in a large crowd. If attending a lady in the evening, it is customary to offer her the arm. If he has the care of two ladies, he should give his arm to but one and they should both walk on the same side of him. It is a very amusing sight to see a gentleman walking between two ladies, a sort of a thorn-between-two-roses affair. When crossing the street with a lady who has his arm, the gentleman does not disengage his arm.

CARRY MOST ARTICLES. When a gentleman is escorting any lady in any public place, it is his duty to insist modestly on carrying any article she may have in her hand. In this connection, permit us to say that a husband should always carry the baby.

TAKE HER TO THE HOSTESS. When accompanying a lady to a party or dance, he should always wait at the head of the stairs for her to come from the dressing-room, and, descending the stairs first, he will be ready to offer his arm in the hall, to escort the lady to the mistress of the house.

ATTEND HER DURING THE PARTY. When she has met with other acquaintances, it is then proper to leave her for awhile, but politeness makes it imperative upon him to attend to her needs, to see that she is entertained, and has an escort to the supper-table, but if she is not either mother, wife, or sister, it is proper for you to wait upon her yourself to the supper-room, and provide whatever she may fancy.

ASSIST UNESCORTED WOMEN. If a gentleman sees a lady whom he does not know, unattended and needing assistance, he should offer his services to her at once. She will readily understand the gentle chivalry which prompts him and will feel that by accepting his kindness she does not place herself in a false light. When a gentleman goes to a ball without a lady, he must place himself at the disposal of the hostess and dance with any ladies she selects for him.

DO NOT ASSIST ESCORTED WOMEN. A gentleman does not attempt to attend to the wants of a lady who already has an escort. It is a piece of impertinence to do so.

A Pleasant Drive

The drive along the river is delightful in Summer—a good New England road, shaded with great branching elms and lithe-limbed river-maples. Receding farther from the city is a two-miles' drive through lovely snatches of pine woods, invitingly cool and quiet. What glossy vines and mossy carpets border the way, and how dreamily, softly, we move along in these hushed places!

—Celia M. French, "Aunt Sally's Home," 1873

OFFER AID WHEN ALIGHTING FROM A CARRIAGE. The gentleman should step out first and then turn and offer the lady both hands, particularly if the vehicle be some distance from the ground.

ASSIST HER WHILE CYCLING. Of course, a gentleman who accompanies a lady is ever on the alert to assist his companion in every possible way. He will, of course, assist her in mounting and dismounting, and, should she be so unfortunate as to take a header, he will soon be at her side to assist her to rise, making himself generally useful and incidentally agreeable. His place on the road is at her left, that he may the more carefully guard her when meeting other cyclers and teams, he risking all danger from collisions.

PART SIX

Miscellaneous Recipes and Remedies

CHAPTER ONE

ℛECIPES FOR GROOMING THE BODY

Skin and Face

TO KEEP HANDS SOFT AND WHITE. A French recipe for this purpose is to sleep in gloves filled with a paste made of ½ pound of soft soap, 1 gill of salad oil, and 1 ounce of mutton tallow. Boil together until thoroughly incorporated. As soon as this is done boiling, but before cold, add 1 gill of spirits of wine and a grain of musk. This is rather a troublesome process, but the result is entirely satisfactory.

TO CURE MOIST HANDS. Some people have moist, clammy hands that are very disagreeable to the touch. Exercise, plain living, and the local application of starch powder and lemon juice will cure this affliction.

TO WHITEN ARMS. For an evening party or theatricals, rub arms with glycerine; and, before the skin has absorbed it all, dust on refined chalk.

TO MAKE COLD CREAM (WHICH ALSO REMOVES FRECKLES). To 1 ounce of white wax melted in a clean dish, put 1 cup of fresh lard, ½ teaspoonful of pulverized gum camphor, and 1 teaspoonful of glycerine; stir well and pour into cups or other molds that have been dipped into cold water. When solid, turn out and wrap in tin foil.

Hood's Olive Ointment

CURES:

CHAPPED LIPS AND HANDS,

HARD AND SOFT CORNS,

INGROWING NAILS, BOILS, BURNS, SORES,

SALT RHEUM OR ECZEMA.

CUTS, FLESH WOUNDS, SCROFULOUS SORES,

PIMPLES, TETTERS, FESTERS, ERUPTIONS,

SORE NIPPLES, BROKEN BREASTE,

BRUISES, INFLAMMATION, PILES, CHILBLAINS,

CUTANEOUS DISEASES, ERUPTIONS,

And the hundred and one things for which a good family salve is constantly used. **HOOD'S OLIVE OINTMENT** is prepared only by C.I. Hood & Co.... Apothecaries. Laboratory: Thorndike Street, Lowell, Mass. Price 25 cents a box; five boxes $1. Sent by mail, on receipt of price, to any address.

—Hood's Cook Book Reprint Number One, 1877

TO REMOVE SKIN TAN. An elegant preparation for removing tan is made of new milk, ½ pint; lemon juice, ¼ ounce; white brandy, ½ ounce. Boil all together and remove scum. Use night and morning.

TO FORTIFY AGAINST WRINKLES. The hand of Time cannot be stayed, but his marks upon the face need not be placed there prematurely. One of the best local treatments consists in bathing the skin frequently in cold water and then rubbing with a towel until the flesh is aglow. A little bran added to the water is a decided improvement.

This treatment stimulates the functions of the skin and gives it vigor. The wrinkling may be further remedied by washing the parts three times a day with a mix of 4 drams glycerine, 2 drams tannin, 2 drams rectified spirits, and 8 ounces water.

Hair

To cleanse the hair. Break the whites of two eggs into a basin of soft water and work them up to a froth in the roots of the hair. Rinse thoroughly with clean warm water.

Hair-curling liquid for ladies. Take borax, 2 ounces; gum Senegal in powder, 1 dram; add hot rater (not boiling), 1 quart Stir, and, as soon as the ingredients are dissolved, add 2 ounces of spirits of wine strongly impregnated with camphor. On retiring to rest, wet the locks with the above liquid, and roll them on twists of paper as usual. Leave them till morning, when they may be unwrapped to form ringlets.

To prevent falling hair and to remove dandruff. A hair-wash for keeping the hair from falling and cleansing it of dandruff is sold by the perfumers and is made as follows: Take castor oil, ½ pound; strongest alcohol, ½ pint; powdered cantharides, 48 grains; oil of bergamot, ½ ounce; attar of roses, 4 drops. Mix, let them stand for seven days, frequently shaking, and then filter and keep in bottles.

To ward off gray hair. We can only counsel moderation in all those pleasures that tend to an exciting, unhealthy mode of living, but here is a recipe that a writer says she believes will prevent graying: melt 4 ounces pure hog's lard (unsalted) and 4 drams spermaceti together, and when cool, add 4 drams oxide of bismuth. Perfume to suit yourself. Use as a dressing.

To prevent baldness. Feather pillows, by conforming to the shape of the head, prevent ventilation and tend to overheat the scalp. This weakens it and may lead to premature baldness or other affliction. Curled hair should be substituted for feathers whenever possible.

TO CURE BALDNESS. The celebrated Baron Dupuytren's pomade, a recipe known for many years, has found a prominent place in the list of remedies for this evil. Leave 6 ounces of boxwood shavings to steep for fourteen days at 60 degrees temperature in 12 ounces of proof spirit. Strain off the liquid and add 2 ounces spirits of rosemary and 1 ½ ounces spirits of nutmeg. Rub this thoroughly on the bald spots, night and morning.

Teeth

TO CARE FOR THE TEETH. Salt and water cure tender gums. In the early stages, vinegar will remove tartar, but if it remains too long it has a tendency to loosen the teeth. Never use a pin or any metal substance to remove food that lodges between the teeth. Food and drinks that are too hot or too cold will destroy the beauty of the teeth.

TO CLEAN THE TEETH. Rub them with the ashes of burnt bread. The juice of the strawberry is a natural dentifrice.

TO FASTEN THE TEETH. Put powdered alum, the quantity of a nutmeg, in a quart of spring water for twenty-four hours, then strain the water and gargle with it.

TO CURE FOUL BREATH. A gargle made of a spoonful of chloride of lime dissolved in a half tumbler of water will sweeten the breath. Bad breath also can be rendered less disagreeable by rinsing the mouth with Horsford's Acid Phosphate.

TO CURE SPECIFIC ODORS. We wish there were some law to prevent people from polluting their breaths with onions and tobacco when they are going into a mixed company. No one has a right to make himself in any manner offensive to others. All the laws of good breeding forbid it. The taint of smoking can be overcome by chewing common parsley. The odor imparted to the breath by garlic and onions may be very much diminished by chewing roasted coffee grains or parsley leaves and seeds.

Soap, Cologne, and Powder

To make fine cologne water. Into a bottle, drop the following oils: 1 dram each of lavender and bergamot, 2 drams each of lemon and rosemary, 8 drams each of cinnamon and cloves, and 50 drams of tincture of musk. Cork and shake well.

To make violet powder. Take 12 pounds of wheat starch and 2 pounds of powdered orris; mix together, and add ½ ounces of attar of lemon and 2 drams each of attars of bergamot and cloves.

To make hard soap. Pour 4 gallons boiling water onto 6 pounds of washing soda and three of unslaked lime. Let it stand until perfectly clear, then drain off. Put in 6 pounds clean fat. Boil until it begins to harden—about two hours—stirring most of the time. While boiling, thin with 2 gallons of cold water, which you have poured on the alkaline mixture after draining off the 4 gallons This must also settle clear before it is drawn off. Add it when there is danger of boiling over. Try the thickness by cooling a little on a plate. Put in a handful of salt just before taking from the fire. Wet a tub to prevent sticking; turn in the soap and let it stand until solid. Cut into bars; put on a board and let it dry. This will make about 40 pounds of nice soap, much better for washing (when it has dried out for two or three months) than yellow turpentine soap.

TO MAKE SOFT SOAP. Let 10 pounds of grease, 6 pounds of washing soda, and 8 gallons of hot water stand for several days until the grease is eaten up. If too thick, add more water. Stir every day. If wood-ashes are used instead of soda, boil the mixture.

Chapter Two

$\mathcal{R}$EMIES FOR ILLNESS

Discontented Babies

To soothe the teething baby. For sleeplessness, irritability, and discomfort accompanying teething, much can be done by the mother:

※ A hot footbath will often have a soothing effect by relieving the congestion in the head and mouth. Mustard can be added with benefit.

※ A good movement of the bowels, induced with castor oil, will relieve congestion in the gums.

※ The mother's finger dipped in syrup of lettuce can be gently carried over the tender and inflamed gum and, now and then, by a little firmer pressure, may allow the point of the tooth to free its way.

※ Make a dried-flour preparation by tying 1 cup of flour into a stout muslin bag and dropping it into cold water. Then set a over the fire. Boil three hours steadily. Turn out the flour ball and dry in the hot sun all day; or, if you need it at once, dry in a moderate oven without shutting the door. To use it, grate 1 tablespoonful for a cupful of boiling milk and water (half and half). Wet up the flour with a very little cold water; stir in, and boil five minutes. Put in a little salt.

To soothe colicky babies. Paregoric, whisky, brandy, or soothing syrup are improper remedies for colic. Drugging the baby into insensibility or making it drunk will not remove the cause of illness. Colic is often a symptom of some other condition, so this condition should be ascertained and treated:

Learn When to Give Medicine and WheN to Wait

❀ For colic that may come from cold hands and feet, keep a flannel belly band on the baby in both summer and winter.

❀ Colic is often due to constipation, in which case an enema of warm water—with the addition of salt at the rate of a level teaspoonful to the pint—is required, followed by 1 or 2 teaspoonsful of castor oil or other gentle laxative medicine.

To help with pneumonia. Garlic, when applied along the spinal column and over the chest of infants in the form of poultice, is very useful.

Sick Children

To remedy a cough or whooping cough:

● Spread butter plentifully on paper (to protect clothing) and lay over the chest, letting it come well up to the throat.

● Administer a syrup formed from sugar and onion juice.

● Rub the feet thoroughly with hog's lard—before the fire, on going to bed—and keep the child warm therein.

- Rub the back, at lying down, with old rum; it seldom fails.
- Give a spoonful of juice of pennyroyal, mixed with brown sugar candy, twice a day.
- Give ½ pint of milk, warm from the cow, with the quantity of a nutmeg of conserve of roses dissolved in it, every morning.
- In desperate cases, change of air will have a good effect.

To prevent croup. Take two skeins of black sewing silk, braid them together so they will wear well, and tie loosely around the neck so it will go below the clothes out of sight; and the child will never have the croup while it is worn. Now, some will laugh at this and call it an old woman's notion, but as it costs but little and can do no harm; if you will only try it, you will save the little ones lots of misery and yourselves many a sleepless night.

Cures the Orphans

The Rev. Mother of the Convent of the Holy Family, Baltic, Conn., writes that she can speak very highly of the Kickapoo Indian Remedies. She always has a supply of each kind on hand the year around. For several years they have stood the test in every case. The health of two hundred children under her care is paramount to everything else. A fever, cold or a cough is seldom known, thanks to the Kickapoo Indian Sagwa, Indian Oil, and Indian Cough Cure, while the Kickapoo Indian Salve and Kickapoo Indian Worm Killer have often proved their effectiveness.

—*Healy & Bigelow's New Cook Book,* 1890

The Midnight Horror   Croup!

CROUP! That vulture of the night which sweeps down upon our little ones sleeping so quietly by our side, and, almost without a moment's warning, bears them from our reach forever—what father, what mother, does not tremble at its name? It chooses the darkness for its ravages, and stealing insidiously upon its victims, suffocates them in our arms almost before their first faint cries for help are heard.

We awake—we find our darling vainly struggling for breath; the harsh, raspin cough strikes terror to our quivering nerves—we are confused, we hesitate, we can think of nothing to do, our reason forsakes us, no physician is near, the deadly membrane is fast cutting off the little one's breath, there is a wheezing, sucking sound as he gasps for life, his strength fails—one feeble word, one pleading look—and our darling is dead—within a few minutes from the first dread signal.

Parents, we know you need never have this experience if you have a bottle of 'Ransom's Hive Syrup and Tolu' in the house, and if you use it according to directions.

—Ransom's Family Receipt Book, 1855

TO TREAT CROUP. The instant croupy threatenings are observed, keep the child indoors and serve very light food indeed—and not much of that—until the symptoms have abated. Put a mustard plaster on the wind-pipe and let it redden the skin, but not blister. Put the feet in mustard water as hot as they can bear it. Then wipe them dry and keep them covered warm. Croup requires very prompt treatment; if home treatment does not relieve, send immediately for a physician.

- ❋ Never lean with the back upon anything that is cold.
- ❋ Never begin a journey until the breakfast has been eaten.
- ❋ Never take warm drinks and then immediately go out in the cold air.
- ❋ Keep the back, especially between the shoulders, well covered; also the chest well protected.
- ❋ In sleeping in a cold room, establish the habit of breathing through the nose, and never with the mouth open.
- ❋ Never go to bed with cold or damp feet; always toast them by a fire 10 or 15 minutes before going to bed.
- ❋ Never omit weekly bathing, for, unless the skin is in active condition, the cold will close the pores and favor congestion or other diseases.
- ❋ After exercise of any kind, never ride in an open carriage or near the window of a car for a moment; it is dangerous to health and even to life.
- ❋ When hoarse, speak as little as possible until it is recovered from, else the voice may be permanently lost or difficulties of the throat be produced.
- ❋ Warm the back by a fire, and never continue keeping the back exposed to heat after it has become comfortably warm; to do otherwise is debilitating.
- ❋ When going from a warm atmosphere into a colder one, keep the mouth closed so that the air may be warmed by its passage through the nose ere it reaches the lungs.

—A.W. Chase, *Dr. Chase's Third Last and Complete Receipt Book and Household Physician,* 1903

To RELIEVE A TOOTHACHE. Cut a large raisin open, roast it or heat it, and apply it around the tooth while it is as hot as can be borne. It will operate like a little poultice and will draw out the inflammation.

To PREVENT SCARLET FEVER. Give, in a dose of as many drops as the years of the child's age, a mixture of extract of belladonna, 3 grains; cinnamon-water, 1 dram; distilled water, 7 drams. Label as poison.

To PREVENT THE RICKETS, TENDERNESS, AND WEAKNESS. Dip children in cold water every morning, at least till they are eight or nine months old. No roller should ever be put round their bodies, nor any stays used. Instead, when they are put into short petticoats, put a waistcoat under their frocks. It is best to wean a child when seven months old. It should lie in the cradle at least a year.

Receipts for Ailing Adults

To REMEDY ALMOST ANYTHING. Break an egg. Separate the yolk and white. Whip each to a stiff froth. Add 1 tablespoonful of arrowroot and a little water to the yolk. Rub till smooth and free from lumps. Pour slowly into ½ pint of boiling water, stirring all the time. Let it simmer till jelly-like. Sweeten to the taste and add 1 tablespoonful of French brandy. Stir in the frothed white and take hot in winter. In summer, set on ice before stirring in the beaten white.

To CURE THE HEART ACHE. Take a piece of the lean of mutton, about the size of a large walnut, put it into the fire and burn it for some time, till it becomes almost reduced to a cinder, then put it into a clean rag and squeeze it until some moisture is expressed, which must be dropped in the ear as hot as the patient can bear.

To PREVENT THE BAD EFFECTS OF DRINKING COLD LIQUORS. Mix brandy or other spirits, 2 ounces with laudanum, 30 drops. Drink immediately as the shivering fit comes on, then lie down for an hour.

To CURE THOSE WHO ARE TOO MUCH ADDICTED TO DRINKING WINE. Put in a sufficient quantity of wine 3 or 4 large eels, which leave

Instaneous Relief for Burns and Scalds

*H*arper's Weekly informs us that a Dr. Waters, of Salem, Mass., in speaking of the new remedy for burns and scalds, before the Massachusetts Dental Society, deliberately dipped a sponge into boiling water and squeezed it over his wrist, producing a sever scald around his arm some two inches wide, and continued the application, despite the suffering, for half a minute. Then he at once sprinkled on the bi-carbonate of soda, and applied the wet cloth, which almost instantly deadened the pain; and on the next day after this single application of the soda, the less injured parts, were practically well, only a slight discoloration being perceptible, the severe portions being healed in a few days, by simply continuing the wet cloth bandage.

—A. W. Chase, *Dr. Chase's Third Last and Complete Receipt Book and Household Physician*, 1903.

there till quite dead. Give that wine to the person you want to reform, and he or she will be so much disgusted with wine, that though they formerly made use of it, they will now have an aversion to it.

TO BIND A CUT. Dissolve ocean salt in a pitcher of water, and rub this on the flesh with a sponge; or apply cobwebs and brown sugar or the dust of tea, applied with laudanum.

TO TREAT A BURN OR SCALD. Cover it with wet linen cloths, pouring on more water without removing them till the pain is alleviated, when pure hog's lard may be applied. Or apply lather of soap from the shaving-cup with the brush to produce relief. White of egg applied in the same way is also a simple and useful dressing. If the shock is great and there is no reaction, administer frequently aromatic of ammonia or a little brandy and water till the patient rallies.

TO TREAT STINGS. Apply soda, hartshorn, or arnica to the stings of wasps, hornets, and bees. Parsley leaves, applied as a fomentation, will also cure the bites or stings of insects.

TO TREAT VENOMOUS BITES. Apply a moderately tight ligature above the bite of a snake. Wash the wound freely with water to encourage bleeding and then cauterize thoroughly. Afterwards apply lint dipped in equal parts of olive-oil and spirits hartshorn; swallow 10 drops dissolved in a wine-glass of water.

TO CURE HEADACHE. The fresh juice of ground ivy snuffed up the nose; giner powder, formed into a plaster with warm water and applied on paper or cloth to the forehead; mustard poultice applied to the nape of the neck; or a footbath, taken for the purpose of drawing the blood from the head, can also relieve aching of the head.

TO CURE A TOOTHACHE. Saturate a piece of wool with a mixture of 6 grains morphia

What the Tongue Tells

If ever I was so far left to myself as to meditate some rash act, I should, before going into the matter, have a look at my tongue. If it was not perfectly clean and moist I should not consider myself perfectly healthy, nor perfectly sane, and would postpone my proceedings in the hope that my worldly prospects would get brighter. The tongue sympathizes with every trifling ailment of body or mind, and more especially with the state of the stomach. I sincerely believe that real comfort can not be secured in this world by any one who does not keep his feet warm, his head cool, and his tongue clean.

—A.W. Chase, *Dr. Chase's Third Last and Complete Receipt Book and Household Physician,* 1903.

and ½ ounce each of tincture of aconite root, chloroform, laudrum, creosote, oil cloves, and cajuput; add as much gum camphor as the chloroform will dissolve. Put it in the hollow tooth, being certain that the cavity is cleaned out. Catnip leaves are also reputed beneficial in toothache when masticated and applied to the decayed tooth.

To remove flatulency after eating. Take a spoonful of the following mixture in a little water as soon after eating as convenient: Magnesia, 3 drams; carbonate of soda, 2 drams, sal-volatile, 4 drams; rose-water, 7 drams. Mix, and shake the bottle before taking a dose.

To allay nausea. Cloves may be used to allay vomiting and sickness at stomach, to stimulate the digestive functions, improve the flavor or operation of other remedies, and prevent their producing sickness.

To relieve dysentery. Steep black or green tea in boiling water and sweeten with loaf-sugar.

Pleasant to Take

Messrs. C.I. Hood & Co.:

Last fall my boy had a humor develop itself around his finger nails which would fester up, become very sore, and the nail come off; finally it left his fingers and went to his nose, first inside, and at last reaching down on the outside of the nostril, near the lip. We used various remedies without benefit. His general health became very much impaired. I went to my family physician (Dr. Green), and he ordered sarsaparilla. I got a bottle of your make (Hood's Sarsaparilla), and in five or six weeks it began to heal and continued to steadily till entirely well, and his sickly, puny look changed to one of vigor and health. He has taken it most of the time since, as I am desirous of eradicating this humor entirely from the blood. It is exceedingly commendatory of your Sarsparilla that it is so pleasant to take that he really likes it and will call for it.

Very truly yours,
John G. Rogers,
(Firm of Stiles, Rogers, & Co.)
Market Street, Lowell, Mass.

—Hood's Cook Book, 1877

TO CURE OBESITY. Fat people may reduce their flesh rapidly by drinking sassafras tea, either cold or hot, with or without sugar. There are conditions of health when it might be injurious, however, and a physician should be consulted before using it. A strong infusion may be made of 1 ounce of sassafras to 1 quart of water. Boil half an hour very slowly, let it cool, and keep from the air.

Miscelleanous Receipts Just for Females

TO SOFTEN HARD BREASTS. Apply turnips roasted till soft, then mashed and mixed with a little oil of roses. Change this twice a day, keeping the breast very warm with flannel.

TO RELIEVE SORE AND SWELLED BREASTS. Boil a handful of chamomile, and as much mallows in milk and water. Foment with it betwveen two flannels, as hot as can be borne, every twelve hours. It also dissolves any knot or swelling in any part where there is no inflammation.

TO CURE CHAPS IN WOMEN'S NIPPLES. Apply balsam of sugar. Or, apply butter of wax, which speedily heals them.

TO FACILITATE CHILD-BIRTH. Some physicians consider drinking ½ pint of elm bark powder boiled in 1 pint of new milk daily, during and after the seventh month of gestation, as advantageous in facilitating and causing an easy delivery.

A Nurse Should See to Her Patient's Comfort

❀ The preparation of the bed is a matter of considerable importance and ought to be attended to during the early part of labor... the foot is preferable because the upper part of the bed is thus kept clean and comfortable for the patient when the labor is over, and because of the help derived from being able to plant the feet firmly against the bed-post during the pains...

❀ *Dress.* As labor advances and it becomes necessary for the patient to be placed in bed, she should put on a clean chemise and night-dress. Amongst the working classes it is still too much the custom for women to be confined in their every-day dress. It is a practice that ought always to be discountenanced.

❀ The hair should be dressed in such a way that the continuous lying in bed after the confinement will not drag upon or entangle it more than is inevitable.

❀ *Company.* It is very undesirable for a woman in labor to be surrounded by a number of friends and neighbors.

❀ *Prophesying.* No nurse should ever allow herself to be teased into prophesying that the labor will be over by a certain hour. If such prophesies turn out incorrect, as they are most likely to do, the patient loses courage and confidence.

❀ All gossip is to be avoided, and nurses should be particularly careful to make no reference to their past experiences, especially such as have been unfavorable. A good, kind nurse will not be at a loss for a few helpful and encouraging words as labor goes on and will not need to have recourse either to foolish promises or dismal anecdotes.

—A.W. Chase, *Dr. Chase's Third Last and Complete Receipt Book and Household Physician,* 1903

⚜ External violence, as kicks or blows, a fall, or violent action, as dancing, riding, jumping, or much walking. Women in the state of pregnancy should avoid many of the domestic operations so proper at other times for good housewives to engage in. As our aim is to be practically useful, we venture, at the risk of exciting a smile, to mention some exertions that ought to be avoided, viz., hanging up curtains, bedmaking, washing...

⚜ Straining of the body, as from coughing

⚜ Costiveness

⚜ Irritation of the neighboring parts, as from severe purging, falling down of the gut, or piles.

⚜ Any sudden or strong emotion of the mind, as fear, joy, surprise.

⚜ The pulling of a tooth has been known to produce a miscarriage; and though toothache is occasionally very troublesome to women in the pregnant state, the operation of drawing teeth should, if possible be avoided a that time

⚜ Women marrying when rather advanced in age are apt to miscarry

⚜ It would be hazardous to name any particular age at which it is too late to marry, but the general observation is worth attending to

⚜ Constitutional debility from ...bleeding or purging; or from disease, as dropsy, fever, small-pox.

⚜ A state the very opposite of this is sometimes the cause of abortion, viz, a robust and vigorous habit with great fullness of blood and activity of the vascular system

⚜ The death of the child.

—A.W. Chase *Dr. Chase's Third Last and Complete Receipt Book and Household Physician,* 1903

CHAPTER THREE

———•———

$\mathcal{H}$OUSEHOLD RECIPES

$\mathcal{R}$emedies for $\mathcal{H}$ousehold $\mathcal{P}$ests

TO RID THE HOME OF INSECTS

-⊨ Dissolve 1 ounce corrosive sublimate in one pint strong spirits. Put it on the bedsteads with a feather, and it will destroy the *bedbugs* and their eggs also. If the scent is not objectionable, 2 ounces commercial carbolic acid will greatly improve the mixture.

-⊨ Cayenne pepper will keep the storeroom and pantry free from *ants* and *cockroaches*.

-⊨ For *bugs and ants*, one may also dissolve 2 pounds alum in 3 quarts boiling water. Apply boiling hot with a brush. Add alum to whitewash for storerooms, pantries, and closets. It is well to pound alum fine and sprinkle it about beds infested with bugs.

-⊨ Kerosene oil is a sure remedy for *red ants*. Place small blocks under a sugar barrel, so as not to let the oil touch the barrel.

-⊨ Uncork a bottle of oil of pennyroyal, and it will drive away *mosquitoes* or other blood-sucking insects; they will not return so long as the scent of it is in the room.

To rid the home of rodents

🙾 Mix a little powdered potash with meal and throw it into the rat-holes and it will not fail to drive the *rats* away.

🙾 If a *mouse* enters into any part of your dwelling, saturate a rag with cayenne in solution and stuff it into his hole.

Cleaning and Polishing Utensils and Furniture

To **make stove blacking**. To make the fine polish given stoves by those skilled in the art, apply a thin mixture of black varnish and turpentine with a paint or varnish brush to a portion of the stove; then with a cloth dust this over with pulverized British luster or stove-polish, which is carburet of iron, in 25-pound packages. The process conducted in this manner is quite brief but gives beautiful results.

To **clean copper ware**. Wash, and rub with half a lemon. Take a handful of common salt, enough vinegar and flour to make a paste; mix together thoroughly. There is nothing better for cleaning coppers. After using the paste, wash thoroughly with hot water, rinse in cold water, and wipe dry.

To **clean enameled ware**. Dampen a cloth, dip it in common soda, rub the ware briskly, wash and wipe dry. Or keep them clean by rubbing with sifted wood ashes or whitening.

To **clean earthenware**. Put in a kettle with cold water, ashes, and sal soda, bring to a boil, and after boiling let stand 24 hours in the lye; or fill the vessels with hot lime water and let them stand 24 hours.

To **repair cracks**. If earthenware or china articles begin to crack, paint the inside of the vessel, especially the cracks, with melted sugar. The syrup will enter the cracks and act as a cement.

To **clean glassware**. Fill with buttermilk, let stand 48 hours, and wash in soapsuds. Or, put in 2 tablespoonsful of vinegar and 1 tablespoonful of baking soda. This will effervesce vigorously. Hold the article over the sink; if a decanter, do not cork or the vessel may burst.

TO CLEAN DRAPERIES. Draperies and tapestries hung upon the walls may be cleaned by pouring gasoline into a shallow pan and brushing them with this by means of a soft brush or whisk broom.

TO POLISH HARDWOOD FLOORS. Chip up fine not quite half a pound of beeswax and put it on the stove to melt. When melted, pour it in one quart of turpentine and add five cents' worth of ammonia. Then set it in a tin pail of hot water and stir the polish over the fire until thoroughly blended. Remember that all these ingredients are highly flammable and guard against their taking fire. See that the hardwood floor is perfectly clean, dry, and free from dust; then apply the polish to it with a soft woolen cloth, rubbing it well into the grain of the wood; next, rub the floor very hard with a polishing-brush. Hardwood floors require polishing two or three times a week.

TO CLEAN FURNITURE. Mix ½ pint linseed oil, ½ pint vinegar, ½ pint turpentine. Apply with a flannel rag and then rub with a dry flannel.

Clothing

TO CLEAN LACE. Stretch the lace carefully on a thick piece of wrapping paper, fastening the edges with pins. Sprinkle it quite thickly with calcined magnesia, cover with another piece of wrapping paper, and place it under a pile of books or other heavy weight for three or four days. The magnesia can then be shaken off, and the lace will appear like new, not only clean, but with edges in perfect condition. Calcinated magnesia is very cheap, and this method is well worth trying.

TO CLEAN DARK OR SOBER-COLORED SILK. Mix together 2 cups cold water, 1 tablespoonful honey, 1 pound soft soap, and 1 wineglass alcohol. Shake up well; lay the silk, a breadth at a time, on a table, and sponge both sides with this, rubbing it well in; shake it about well and up and down in a tub of cold water; flap it as dry as you can, but do not wring it. Hang it by the edges, not the middle, until fit to iron.

TO CLEAN DOUBTFUL CALICOES. Put 1 teaspoonful of sugar of lead into a pailful of water and soak 15 minutes before washing.

To CLEAN CREPE, MOURN-
ING, AND OTHER BLACK
GOODS. Black dress goods
may be washed by observing
the same caution as for other
colored fabrics, whether cotton, linen, wool, or silk. Use 2
tablespoonsful of ammonia to
½ gallon of water. Take a piece
of black cloth and sponge off
with the preparation and afterward with clean water. Iron
while damp on the wrong side,
or that which is to be inside
when the stuff is made up.

To CLEAN DELICATE STRAW
GOODS. Straws such as Milan
and Leghorn can be thor-
oughly cleaned by mixing the
juice of a lemon with 1 tablespoonful of powdered sulphur
to form a thick paste. Apply
this to the hat with a nail-
brush or toothbrush, first removing the band, and rub the
paste thoroughly into the
straw. Afterwards, rinse by
dashing water upon it from a
glass, but without soaking.
Shape the hat while still damp
with a warm iron, pressing
through a wet cloth until dry.
Or press into shape and dry
out of doors in the sun

Moth Powder

To make moth powder to put
away furs, woolens, etc.:

Mix thoroughly 1 dram
lupulin (flour of hops), 2 ounces
Scotch snuff, 1 ounce each,
powdered gum camphor and
black pepper, and 4 ounces
cedar sawdust. Strew (or put in
small paper bags) among the
furs or woolen goods (after they
have been thoroughly whipped
with small rods) which are
being put away. This powder
contains some of all the best-
know preventives. But if moth
eggs have already been laid in
them, unless the whipping takes
them out, they will hatch and
start their destructive work, unless the benzine or some other
"killer" is used; hence it is best
to keep an eye on them occasionally, and whip thoroughly
again if any are seen. If you shut
moths out, and shut none in,
you are perfectly safe.

—The Boston Transcript,
as relayed in *Dr. Chase's Third Last
and Complete Receipt Book and
Household Physician* , 1903

≋ BIBLIOGRAPHY

BOOKS AND ARTICLES

A Lady of Charleston. *The Carolina Housewife or House and Home.* Charleston, S.C.: W.R. Babcock & Co, 1847.

American Stove Co., Publishers. *Cook Book: "New Process" Wick Oil Cook Stove.* American Stove Co., Publishers, ca. 1910. At: Emergence of Advertising in America: 1850–1920 (see websites).

Armour and Company, Publishers. *"Pastry Wrinkles" Containing a Few Practical Suggestions on the Use of the New and Better Shortener, Armour's "Simon Pure" Leaf Lard.* Chicago: Armour and Company, 1906. At: Emergence of Advertising in America: 1850–1920 (see websites).

"Bathing," *Peterson's Magazine*, June 1872. At: American Federation of Old West Reenactors (see websites).

Beebe, Katherine. *Home Occupations for Little Children.* Chicago: The Werner Company, 1896.

Beecher, Catherine E., and Harriet Beecher Stowe. *The American Woman's Home, or Principles of Domestic Science.* New York: J.B. Ford, 1869.

California Fruit Growers Exchange, Publishers. *Recipes for Dainty Dishes: Culinary Toilet, and Medicinal Hints.* California Fruit Growers Exchange, ca. 1910s. At: Emergence of Advertising in America: 1850–1920 (see websites).

"Calling Card Etiquette," *The Delineator.* At: Victoriana.Com Study Center, (see websites).

Carnegie, Andrew. "Wealth," *North American Review*, Vol. CXLVII, no. 391 (June 1889), 653–64. At: Internet Modern History Sourcebook (see websites).

Carter, Mary Elizabeth. *Millionaire Households and Their Domestic Economy: With Hints upon Fine Living*. New York: D. Appleton & Co, 1903.

Chase, A.W., M.D. *Dr. Chase's Third Last and Complete Receipt Book and Household Physician (Memorial Edition)*. Detroit: F.B. Dickerson Company, 1903.

Church & Dwight Co., Publishers. *Cow Brand Soda Cook Book and Facts Worth Knowing, Established Half a Century*. N. Y.: Church & Dwight Co., 1900. At: Emergence of Advertising in America: 1850–1920 (see websites).

C. I. Hood & Co. Apothecaries, Publishers. *Hood's Cook Book Reprint Number One*. Lowell, MA: C. I. Hood & Co., post 1877. At: Emergence of Advertising in America: 1850–1920 (see websites).

Corson, Juliet. *Miss Corson's Practical American Cookery and Household Management*. New York: Dodd, Mead, and Company, 1885.

Craik, Dinah Maria Mulock. *A Woman's Thoughts About Women*. London: Hurst and Blackett, 1858. At: Victorian Women Writers Project (see websites).

Crane, Rev. Jonathan Townley. *Popular Amusements*. Cincinnati: Hitchcock and Walden, 1870. At: Making of America (see websites).

Davis, Rebecca Harding. *Bits of Gossip*. Boston and New York: Houghton, Mifflin & Company and Cambridge: The Riverside Press, 1904. At: University of North Carolina's Documenting the American South Collection (see websites).

Dick & Fitzgerald, Publishers. *Athletic Sports for Boys: A Repository of Graceful Recreations for Youth*. New York: Dick & Fitzgerald, 1866. At: Making of America (see websites).

D. Ransom, Son & Co., Publishers. *Ransom's Family Receipt Book*. Buffalo, N. Y.: D. Ransom, Son & Co.: 1885. At: Emergence of Advertising in America: 1850–1920 (see websites).

Drew, Grace E. "Art and Fashion in Dinner-Giving," *Godey's Lady's Book*, December 1896. At: Godey's Archive: Home and Household Arts Archive (see websites).

Eaton, Seymour. *One Hundred Lessons in Business.* Boston: Seymour Eaton, 1887.

Eaton, Seymour. "'Slips of Tongue and Pen,' Lesson No. 28," *Self-Help and Home-Study,* Vol. 1, No. 5, Boston: Seymour Eaton, January, 1898.

Farmer, Fannie Merritt. *Catering for Special Occasions.* Philadelphia: David McKay, 1911.

Farmer, Fannie Merritt. *The Boston Cooking-School Cook Book.* Boston: Little, Brown, and Company, 1896. Reprint, Mineola, NY: Dover Publications, Inc., 1997.

"Fashions in Calling Cards," *Harper's Bazar,* 1868. At: Victoriana.Com Study Center (see websites).

Fowler, Prof. O.S. "Posture and Kindred Signs Express Existing Sexual States," *Private Lectures on Perfect Men, Women and Children,* 1880. At: Victoriana.Com Study Center (see websites).

French, Celia M. "Aunt Sally's Home," *Ladies' Repository: A Monthly Periodical, Devoted to Literature, Arts, and Religion,* Vol. 11, Issue 2. Cincinnati: Methodist Episcopal Church, 1873. At: Making of America (see websites).

Gardner, Mrs. H.C., "How My Old Silk Was Made Over," *The Ladies Repository: A Monthly Periodical Devoted to Literature, Arts, and Religion,* Vol. 3, Issue 1. Cincinnati: Methodist Episcopal Church, January 1876. At: Making of America (see websites).

Gillette, Mrs. F.L., and Hugo Ziemann. *The White House Cook Book.* Chicago: The Werner Company, 1887. Reprint, Ottenheimer Publishers, Inc., 1999.

Haliburton, Thomas Chandler as Sam Slick [pseud.]. *The Letter-Bag of the Great Western.* New York: G. Routledge and Sons, 1873. At: Making of America (see websites).

Hammond, S. H. and L. W. Mansfield. *Country Margins and Rambles of a Journalist,* New York: J.C. Derby, 1855. At: The On-Line Books Page (see websites).

Harland, Marion. *Common Sense in the Household: A Manual of Practical Housewifery.* New York: Charles Scribner & Co., 1871.

Harper & Brothers, Publishers. "Cotton for Dresses," *Harper's New Monthly Magazine*, Vol. XXXVI (December 1867–May 1868), 611–12, New York: Harper & Brothers, Publishers, 1868.

Harper & Brothers, Publishers. "Editor's Drawer," *Harper's New Monthly Magazine*, Vol. XXXVI (December, 1867–May, 1868), 266, 673. New York: Harper & Brothers, Publishers, 1868.

Harper & Brothers, Publishers. "Etiquette," *Harper's New Monthly Magazine*, Vol. XXXVI (December 1867–May 1868), 384–87. New York: Harper & Brothers, Publishers, 1868.

Hartshorne, Henry, M.D. *The Household Cyclopedia of General Information Containing over Ten Thousand Receipts in All the Useful and Domestic Arts.* Philadelphia: T. Ellwood Zell and Pittsfield, MA: J. Brainard Clarke, 1871.

Hayes, Rutherford B. White House Diary Entry, March 18, 1878. At: The Ohio Historical Society (see websites).

Healy & Bigelow, Publishers. *Healy & Bigelow's New Cook Book.* New Haven, Conn.: Healy & Bigelow, 1890. At: Emergence of Advertising in America: 1850–1920 (see websites).

Heywood, Ezra. "Uncivil Liberty: An Essay to Show the Injustice and Impolicy of Ruling Woman Without Her Consent, *The Word,* 1873.

Huntington, Emily. *The Cooking Garden: A Systematized Course of Cooking for Pupils of All Ages, Including Plan of Work, Bills of Fare, Songs, and Letters of Information.* New York: Trow's Printing and Bookbinding Company, 1885.

The Huntington Herald, Publishers. *The Neighborhood Cook Book: Huntington, Mass., 1897.* Huntington, MA.: Press of *The Huntington Herald,* 1897.

International Health Resort, Publishers. *International Health Resort Recipes,* Chicago: International Health Resort, ca. 1900. At: Emergence of Advertising in America: 1850–1920 (see websites).

J.D. Larkin & Co., Publishers. *Sweet Home Cook Book.* Buffalo, N.Y., 1888. Reprint, Paducah, KY: Image Graphics, Inc.

Jeffries, Prof. B.G., and J.L. Nichols. *The Household Guide or Domestic Cyclopedia.* Naperville, IL: J.L. Nichols & Co., 1898.

Jeremiah Curtis & Sons and John I. Brown & Sons, Publishers. *Mrs. Winslow's Domestic Receipt Book.* Boston: Jeremiah Curtis & Sons and London: John I. Brown & Sons, 1877. At: Emergence of Advertising in America: 1850–1920 (see websites).

Johnson, Helen Louise. *The Enterprising Housekeeper, Suggestions for Breakfast, Luncheon, and Supper 2nd ed.* Philadelphia: The Enterprise Manufacturing Co., 1898. At: Emergence of Advertising in America: 1850–1920 (see websites).

Johnson, Sophia Orne as Daisy Eyebright[pseud.]. *A Manual of Etiquette with Hints on Politeness and Good Breeding.* Philadelphia: David McKay, Publisher, 1873. At: A Celebration of Women Writers (see websites).

Julius Ives & Co., Publishers. *Catalogue.* New York: Julius Ives & Co., 1867.

Junior Group of Hannah Winthrop Chapter, Daughters of the American Revolution. *Favorite Recipes of Famous 'Daughters.'* Cambridge, Massachusetts, ca. 1950.

"Kerosene Lamp Explosion," *Newburyport (MA)Herald.* Reprint, *Scientific American,* September 1867, 193.

Kirkpatrick, Mrs. T.J. *The Housekeepers New Cook Book.* Springfield, OH: Mast, Crowell & Kirkpatrick, 1883.

Knox & Co., Publishers. "Dinner Menu: Horticultural Dining Rooms, No. 61 Bromfield St., Boston," Boston: Knox & Co., 1896. At: American Memory Printed Ephemera Collection (see websites).

Ladies Association of The First Presbyterian Church. *The First Texas Cookbook.* Houston, TX: 1883. Reprint, *The First Texas Cookbook—A Thorough Treatise on the Art of Cookery in 1883.* Austin, TX: Eakin Publications, Inc., 1986.

Ladies of the Guild of St. James' Parish Church, Peace Valley, KY. *Favorite Food of Famous Folk.* Louisville, KY: The Guild of St. James' Parish, 1900.

Ladies of the M.E. Church. *Grayville Cook Book.* Grayville, IL: The Ladies of the M. E. Church, 1912.

Lincoln, Mrs. D.A. *Frozen Dainties (Fifty Choice Receipts for Ice-Creams, Frozen Puddings, Frozen Fruits, Frozen Beverages, Sherbets, and Water Ices).*

Nashua, N. H.: The White Mountain Freezer Co., 1899. At: Emergence of Advertising in America: 1850–1920 (see websites).

Lincoln, Mrs. D.A. *Mrs. Lincoln's Boston Cook Book: What to Do and What Not to Do in Cooking.* Boston: Roberts Brothers, 1884. Reprint, *Boston Cooking School Cook Book—Mrs. D.A. Lincoln—A Reprint of the 1884 Classic.* Mineola, NY: Dover, 1996.

Lincoln, Mrs. Mary J., Lida Ames Willis, Mrs. Sarah Tyson Rorer, Mrs. Helen Armstrong, and Marion Harland. *Home Helps, A Pure Food Cook Book A Useful Collection of Up-to-Date, Practical Recipes by Five of the Leading Culinary Experts in the United States.* Chicago, New York, St. Louis, New Orleans and Montreal: The N.K. Fairbank Company, 1910. At: Emergence of Advertising in America: 1850–1920 (see websites).

Livingston, A.W. *Livingston and the Tomato.* Columbus, Ohio: A.W. Livingston's Sons, Seedmen, 1893. Reprint, with a foreword and appendix by Andrew F. Smith. Columbus: Ohio State University Press, 1998.

Mallon, Isabel A., "The Small Belongings of Dress," *The Ladies' Home Journal,* April 1894. At: The Costume Gallery (see websites).

Mallon, Isabel A. "The Woman of Forty," *The Ladies' Home Journal,* vol. X, no. 10 (September 1893), 19.

Massachusetts Reform Club, Publishers. "Menu and Speech from a meeting held September 28, 1899 at Young's Hotel" Boston: Massachusetts Reform Club. At: American Memory Printed Ephemera Collection (see websites).

Michigan Stove Company, Publishers. *Cupid at Home in the Kitchen.* Detroit and Chicago: The Michigan Stove Company, ca. 1910. At: Emergence of Advertising in America: 1850–1920 (see websites).

Molly Varnum Chapter of the Daughters of the American Revolution, Publishers. *Our Cook Book.* Lowell, MA: Molly Varnum Chapter, 1910.

"Mourning and Funeral Usages," *Harper's Bazar,* April 17, 1886. At: Victoriana.Com Study Center (see websites).

Natural Food Company, Publishers. *The Vital Question Cook Book, The "Vital Question" Being a Discussion of the Food Problem and its Relation to Health and Happiness Including a Comprehensive Treatise on the Principles of Cook-*

ery With Practical And Economical Recipes For Making Simple, Palatable and Nutritious Shredded Wheat Dishes. Niagara Falls, N. Y.: 1908. At: Emergence of Advertising in America: 1850–1920 (see websites).

"New Cotillion Favors for the Season," Harper's Bazar, October, 14, 1899. At: Victoriana.Com Study Center (see websites).

O'Rell, Max. "Petticoat Governments," The North American Review, Volume 163, Issue 476 (July 1896). Cedar Falls, Iowa: University of Northern Iowa. At: Making of America (see websites).

"Our Country Friends," The Lady's Friend, May 1868. At: American Federation of Old West Re-Enactors (see websites).

"Our New Cook Book," Peterson's Magazine, Vol. LIII, No. 3 (March 1868). Philadelphia, PA. At: Victoriana.Com Study Center (see websites).

The Picayune. The Picayune's Creole Cook Book, 2nd ed. New Orleans, LA: The Picayune, 1901.

Plymouth Antiquarian Society. The Plimoth Colony Cook Book. Plymouth, MA: Plymouth Antiquarian Society, 1981.

"Practical Hints for the Household: The Amateur Housekeeper," Godey's Lady's Book, August, 1886. At: Victorian Women's World.

Price Flavoring Extract Co., Publishers. Dr. Price's Delicious Desserts. Chicago: Price Flavoring Extract Co., 1904. At: Emergence of Advertising in America: 1850–1920 (see websites).

"Quotation by Worth," Harper's Bazar, December 15, 1877. At Victoriana.Com Study Center (see websites).

Rorer, Sarah Tyson. Cereal Foods and How to Cook Them. Chicago: American Cereal Company, 1899. At: Emergence of Advertising in America: 1850–1920 (see websites).

Rowland, Mabel. Celebrated Actor Folks' Cookeries: A Collection of the Favorite Foods of Famous Players. New York City: Mabel Rowland, Inc., 1916.

Sargent & Company, Publishers. Gem Chopper Cook Book. Sargent & Company, 1902. At: Emergence of Advertising in America: 1850–1920 (see websites).

Sears, Roebuck and Co., Publishers. *"Kook Kwick" Pressure Cooker Recipes.* Sears, Roebuck and Co., ca 1910s. At: Emergence of Advertising in America: 1850–1920 (see websites).

Seely, Mrs. L. *Mrs. Seely's Cook Book: A Manual of French and American Cookery.* New York: The MacMillan Company, 1902.

Sloan, Dr. Earl S. *Sloan's Cook Book and Advice to Housekeepers (Recipes and Advertisements for Remedies Manufactured by Dr. Earl S. Sloan at 615 Albany Street and 111 East Brookline Street, Boston).* Boston: F. E. Bacon & Co. Printers, 1905. At: Emergence of Advertising in America: 1850–1920 (see websites).

Smith, Jacqueline Harrison and Sue Mason Maury Halsey. *Famous Old Receipts Used a Hundred Years and More in the Kitchens of the North and the South: Contributed by Descendants.* Philadelphia: The John C. Winston Co., 1906.

Smith, Matthew Hale, as Burleigh [pseud.]. *The Old Colony Railroad: Its Connections, Popular Resorts, and Fashionable Watering-Places.* Boston: Rand, Avery, & Co., 1875. At: The On-Line Books Page (see websites).

Stall, Sylvanus, D.D. *What a Young Man Ought to Know.* Philadelphia: The Vir Publishing Company, 1904.

Stoddard, Elizabeth. "The Tea-Party," *Appletons Journal: A Magazine of General Literature,* Vol. 6, Is. 132 (October 7, 1871). New York: D. Appleton and Company. At: Making of America (see websites).

Stowe, Harriet Beecher. *House and Home Papers.* Boston: Fields, Osgood, & Co, 1869. At: Making of America (see websites).

Stratton, Florence. *Favorite Recipes of Famous Women.* New York: Harper, 1925.

"Styles of the Month for Children," *McCall's Magazine,* Vol. XXXV, No. 9 (May 1908). At: The Costume Gallery (see websites).

Swift & Company, Publishers. *The Kitchen Encyclopedia.* Swift & Company, 1911. At: Emergence of Advertising in America: 1850–1920 (see websites).

"Table Manners," *The Ladies' Repository: A Monthly Periodical, Devoted to Literature, Arts, and Religion,* Vol. 25, Is. 2 (February, 1865). Cincinnati: Methodist Episcopal Church. At: Making of America.

Tyree, Marion Cabell. *Housekeeping in Old Virginia*. Louisville, KY: John P. Morton & Co., 1879.

"Victorian Era Etiquette." At: Tamara's Victorian Corner (see websites).

Vincent, Marvin Richardson. *Amusement: A Force in Christian Training*. Troy, NY: W.H. Young, 1867. At: Making of America (see websites).

Vollrath Co., Publishers. *Cuisine.* Wisconsin: Vollrath Co., 1912. At: Emergence of Advertising in America: 1850–1920 (see websites).

Wallace, Lily Haxworth. *The Rumford Complete Cook Book*. Providence, RI: Rumford Chemical Works, 1908.

West, Lucy Scott. *Journal Account of Stay at Rutherford White House, February 16–March 19, 1878*. At: Rutherford B. Hayes Presidential Center (see websites).

White, Mrs. Anna R. *Youth's Educator for Home and Society*. Chicago: Union Publishing House, 1896. At: Rochester History Department's Youth's Educator for Home and Society Page (see websites).

Willard, Frances E. *A Wheel Within a Wheel: How I Learned to Ride the Bicycle (With Some Reflections by the Way)*. Fleming H. Revell Co., 1895. Reprint, Bedford, MA: Applewood Books.

W. M. Underwood Co., Publishers. *Taste the Taste and Some Cookery News*. Boston: W. M. Underwood Co., ca 1910. At: Emergence of Advertising in America: 1850–1920 (see websites).

Women of the First Congregational Church of Marysville, Ohio. *Centennial Buckeye Cook Book*. Marysville, OH: J.H. Shearer & Son, 1876. Reprint, *Centennial Buckeye Cook Book Originally Published in 1876,* with an introduction and appendixes by Andrew F. Smith, Columbus: Ohio State University Press, 2000.

The Woman's Book, vol. 2. New York: Charles Scribner's Sons, 1894.

Wright, A.S. *Wright's Book of 3,000 Practical Receipts*. New York: Dick & Fitzgerald, 1869. At: Making of America (see websites).

WEBSITES

19th Century America
http://members.aol.com/Tchrfromoz/19thcent.html

19th Century American Literary, Historical, and Cultural Studies
www.wsu.edu/~amerstu/19th/19th.html

19th Century Harpers Bazar Magazine
www.victoriana.com/library/harpers/harpers.html

19th Century Scientific American Online
www.history.rochester.edu/Scientific_American

American Federation of Old West Reenactors   www.afowr.com

American Memory: Historical Collections for the National Digital Library
http://memory.loc.gov/ammem/amhome.html

American Memory Printed Ephemera Collection
http://lcweb2.loc.gov/ammem/rbpehtml/—part

American Women's History: A Guide to Resources and Research on the
    Web   http://web.uccs.edu/~history/index/women.html#home

Amherst Common/Interactive Tour/Emily Dickinson
http://www.amherstcommon.com/walking_tour/emily.html

A Celebration of Women Writers
http://digital.library.upenn.edu/women/writers.html

The Costume Gallery   www.costumegallery.com

Diary and Letters of Rutherford B. Hayes
http://www.ohiohistory.org/onlinedoc/hayes/index.cfm

Documenting the American South collection of the University of North
    Carolina at Chapel Hill Academic Affairs Library
http://docsouth.unc.edu/

Emergence of Advertising in America: 1850–1920, featuring the works from
    the Hartman Center for Sales, Advertising & Marketing History; Rare
    Book, Manuscript, and Special Collections Library; Duke University,

Durham, North Carolina; including the Nicole DiBona Peterson Cookbook Collection.   Cookbook Collection
http://scriptorium.lib.duke.edu/eaa/

Godey's Archive: Home and Household Arts Archive
www.spiritone.com/~zsk/hartarch.htm

Godey's Lady's Book
http://www.uvm.edu/~hag/godey/

Godey's Lady's Book On-Liny
http://www.history.rochester.edu/godeys/

Hayes Presidential Center Website, Rutherford B. Hayes' Diary
www.rbhayes.org

Her Heritage
www.plgrm.com/Heritage/women/

The Household Cyclopedia
http://members.nbci.com/mspong/contents.html

Internet Modern History Sourcebook
www.fordham.edu/halsall/mod/modsbook.html

Making of America Project
http://moa.umdl.umich.edu
http://moa.cit.cornell.edu/moa/index.html

Matilda Joslyn Gage Website: Links to Websites on Women in the 19th Century
www.pinn.net/~sunshine/gage/features/gage_lnk.html

Miss Abigail's Time Warp Advice: Old Advice for Contemporary Dilemmas
www.missabigail.com

The Ohio Historical Society
www.ohiohistory.org

The On-Line Books Pagy
http://digital.library.upenn.edu/books

Penn Library Exhibitions
www.library.upenn.edu/special/gallery/aresty/aresty22.html

Pilgrim New Media
www.plgrm.com

Rochester History Department's Youth's Educator for Home and Society
Page   www.history.rochester.edu/ehp-book/yefhas

Rutgers University Library: Nineteenth Century
www.libraries.rutgers.edu/rul/rr_gateway/research_guides/history/
texts_by_period.shtml#19c1800s

Tamara's Victorian Corner (see websites).
www.geocities.com/Paris/Opera/1829/ettiquette.html

University of North Carolina at Chapel Hill Libraries Documenting the
American South Collection
http://docsouth.unc.edu/southlit/southlit.html

Victorian Women's World   www.spiritone.com/~zsk/index.htm

Victorian Women Writers Project
www.indiana.edu/~letrs/vwwp/index.html

Victoriana.Com Study Center   www.victoriana.com

Household Words: Women Write for and from the Kitchen, featuring the
collection of the Walter H. & Leonore Annenberg Rare Book & Manuscript Library of the University of Pennsylvania.
www.library.upenn.edu/special/gallery/aresty/aresty22.html

INDEX